John Paul Jones

American Naval Hero

Leaders of the American Revolution

Leaders of the American Revolution

John Paul Jones

American Naval Hero

Liz Sonneborn

CHELSEA HOUSE
PUBLISHERS
A Haights Cross Communications Company ®
Philadelphia

CHELSEA HOUSE PUBLISHERS
VP, New Product Development Sally Cheney
Director of Production Kim Shinners
Creative Manager Takeshi Takahashi
Manufacturing Manager Diann Grasse

Staff for John Paul Jones
Executive Editor Lee Marcott
Editorial Assistant Carla Greenberg
Production Editor Bonnie Cohen
Photo Editor Sarah Bloom
Cover and Interior Designer Keith Trego
Layout 21st Century Publishing and Communications, Inc.

A Haights Cross Communications ✦ Company ®

www.chelseahouse.com

First Printing

9 8 7 6 5 4 3 2 1

Library of Congress Cataloging-in-Publication Data

Sonneborn, Liz.
   John Paul Jones: American naval hero/Liz Sonneborn
      p. cm.—(Leaders of the American Revolution)
   Includes bibliographical references and index.
   ISBN 0-7910-8621-6 (hard cover)
   1. Jones, John Paul, 1747–1792—Juvenile literature. 2. Admirals—United
States—Biography—Juvenile literature. 3. United States—Navy—Biography—
Juvenile literature. 4. United States—History—Revolution, 1775–1783—Navel
operations—Juvenile literature. I. Title. II. Series.
E207.J7S76 2006
973.3'5'092—dc22
                                                            2005004785

38888000193601

Contents

A Duel
at Sea

On September 23, 1779, the *Bonhomme Richard* was sailing near Flamborough Head on the eastern coast of England. John Paul Jones, the ship's captain, was on deck, keeping watch, although all seemed quiet. The wind was light, and the water was calm.

Suddenly, far in the distance, something caught Jones's eye. Through his spyglass, he could see a tall ship about ten miles away. Soon, Jones could make out dozens of smaller ships sailing nearby. It was a thrilling sight. As he studied the ships in front of him, he declared to a midshipman, "This is the very fleet which I have been so long cruising for."[1]

Jones had already spent four years as a captain in the American navy. Although born in Scotland, he had eagerly joined the American colonists in fighting for their independence from British rule. But, for the most part, the American Revolution was being fought on land. The American navy had few ships. Those it did have were old and slow—hardly a match for the mighty British navy's fleet of combat ships.

Even so, Jones had earned a reputation as a fierce war captain. He had captured many British merchant ships and invaded a town along the coast of England. But Jones longed to go to battle with a great English warship. When he saw the British ships off Flamborough, he knew that his chance had finally come.

THE *SERAPIS*

As the *Bonhomme Richard* slowly glided toward the

enemy vessels, Jones sized up the situation. He saw two warships. The smaller one, the *Countess of Scarborough,* was lightly armed and posed little threat. The larger one was the *Serapis.* It was captained by Richard Pearson, who had had a distinguished 30-year career at sea. Recently built, the *Serapis* was a fast ship. Jones knew it would be easy for Pearson to maneuver. In addition, Pearson's ship was equipped with 44 guns. Jones's *Bonhomme Richard* had only 40 guns, and many of them were so old he could not be sure they would fire properly.

The dozens of vessels traveling with the two British warships were merchant ships. They were carrying canvas, lumber, and other goods from Scandinavia. The *Serapis* and *Countess of Scarborough* were guarding these ships to make sure that their valuable cargo arrived safely in England. If Jones could defeat the *Serapis,* he could seize these goods for the Americans.

Jones was confident that he could win a battle with the *Serapis.* The British ship was undoubtedly more seaworthy than his own *Bonhomme Richard.* But Jones was traveling with three other warships—the *Alliance,* the *Pallas,* and the *Vengeance.* Because of their large size, the four American ships had a great advantage over the two British vessels. Jones believed that if his ships could position themselves on either side of the *Serapis,* they could pound it with cannonfire, completely disabling it almost as soon as the fighting began.

At five o'clock, Jones was ready to prepare for battle. He told his drummers to "beat to quarters." They drummed a signal for all aboard to man their battle stations. Sailors ran to clear the deck of chairs, tables, and anything else that might send off splinters if hit. They poured sand everywhere. It would absorb blood, keeping the deck from getting too slippery in the heat of the fray. Below deck, the ship's surgeon gathered the tools of his trade, including a saw to cut off wounded limbs and a bucket to stash them in.

Within an hour, Jones was ready to charge toward the *Serapis.* He signaled the other American ships to follow. However, Jones soon realized that they were hanging back as he raced ahead. Maybe his fellow captains could not see his signal through the low light of dusk. Maybe they were just ignoring him, reluctant to battle the powerful British fleet. Whatever their reasons, one thing was clear—the *Bonhomme Richard* was taking on the *Serapis* alone.

Although born in Scotland, John Paul Jones joined the colonists in their fight for independence from Britain, serving as a captain in the American navy.

In an instant, Jones's chance for a victory went from a sure thing to a long shot.

As Jones's ship charged ahead, he spied Pearson, wearing a bright blue coat with gold trim, on the *Serapis*'s deck. The British captain was nailing a flag adorned with the symbol of the British navy to a pole. A flag was normally hoisted on a tall staff, where it waved throughout a battle. If a captain wanted to surrender, he brought down, or struck, the flag to signal the enemy. By nailing up the flag, Pearson was sending a message to his crew. He was telling them that, no matter what, no one was to strike the flag. This was going to be a fight to the death.

When the two ships got close enough, Pearson shouted out, "What ship is that?" Jones had one of his men answer, "*Princess Royal.*" The *Princess Royal* was a British ship. Jones hoped that his lie would make Pearson drop his guard. But Pearson was not so easily fooled. He threatened to start firing unless they told him the real name of their ship and the country it was from.

Before Pearson got his answer, a shot rang out. One of Jones's men had panicked and fired his musket. A moment later, the air was full of the sound of gunfire.

Only 25 yards apart, both ships were wracked by cannonballs and bullets. Men lay dead, while the wounded screamed for help. The less-experienced crew of the *Bonhomme Richard* was especially devastated. As midshipman Nathaniel Fanning later remembered, "[The *Serapis*] made a dreadful havoc of our crew. Men were falling all parts of the ship by the *scores.*"[2]

As the battle continued, Pearson handled his ship masterfully. Repeatedly, he maneuvered it to its best advantage, allowing his men to hammer away at the *Bonhomme Richard* again and again. Despite Jones's best efforts, his men were being slaughtered, and his ship was being destroyed.

Still determined to win, Jones tried to move his ship at a right angle to the *Serapis* so that he could shoot cannonballs down the length of the British ship. But, by this point, the *Bonhomme Richard* was almost impossible to steer. It stalled in front of the *Serapis*. Pearson tried to turn his ship away, but it was too late. The *Serapis* rammed right into the side of the American ship.

"I HAVE NOT YET BEGUN TO FIGHT"

Jones saw an opportunity in the disaster. He ordered his men to lash together the two ships' masts—the high vertical poles that supported their sails. The Americans then threw grappling hooks onto the deck of the *Serapis,* to ensure that the British could not get away. Side by side, the two ships fired away, filling the sky with thick yellow smoke. Out of the haze, the *Alliance* suddenly appeared and opened fire. Its wild shots struck not only the *Serapis* but also the *Bonhomme Richard.* Jones's men screamed out "Wrong ship!" and begged the American vessel to stop its reckless attack.

Water started to pour into the *Bonhomme Richard.* Convinced that the ship was sinking and sure that Jones was dead, two mates cried out "Quarters!" in order to surrender to the British. As they rushed to strike the American flag, they heard Jones screaming, "Who are those rascals? Shoot them! Kill them!" Emerging out of the smoke, he lunged for the mates. He tried to shoot one, but his gun did not fire. Jones then hurled his weapon at the other mate, striking him in the head.

Pearson rushed to the railing of the *Serapis.* "Have you struck? Do you call for Quarters?" he screamed over the roar of gunfire. In Jones's own official report of the battle, he wrote that he responded "in the most

The battle between the *Bonhomme Richard* and the *Serapis* lasted for hours as the damaged ships exchanged fire.

determined negative."[3] But an eyewitness told an early biographer of Jones that the captain shouted back, "I have not yet begun to fight." It is not clear whether Jones spoke these exact words. Nevertheless, this famous declaration of defiance has been associated with Jones ever since.

The furious fighting continued. The British tried to board the *Bonhomme Richard,* but the Americans charged them with such ferocity that they had to make a quick retreat. The *Alliance* reappeared and once again shot at both ships. Then, a little after ten o'clock, the battle began to turn. One crewman, carrying a bucket of grenades, managed to climb the mainsail yard, the horizontal pole from which the largest sail was hung. Leaning over the deck of the *Serapis,* he hurled a grenade into an open hatch, which set off a series of explosions inside the enemy ship.

Pearson reappeared on deck. Half his men were dead, and his ship was ablaze. Amidst the chaos, the British captain called out to Jones, "Sir, I have struck! I ask for quarter!" Pearson himself then ripped down the now shredded British flag from the post where he had nailed it only hours before.

Jones had won. Against all the odds, his *Bonhomme Richard* was able to overtake a British combat ship.

Jones fought other sea battles during the war. But it was the battle off Flamborough that assured his place in history as the greatest naval hero of the American Revolution.

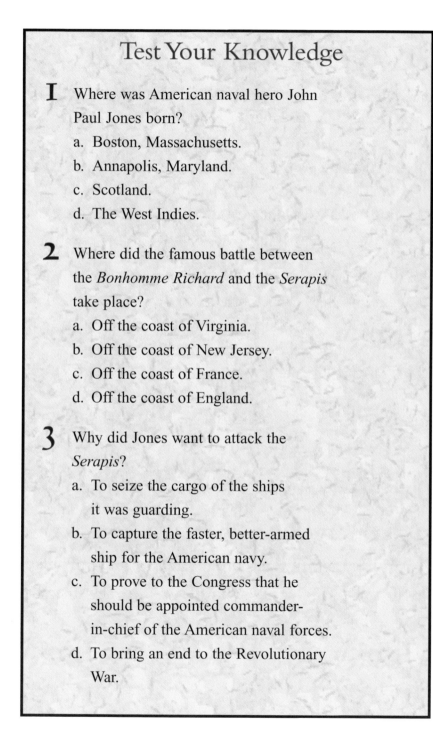

Test Your Knowledge

I Where was American naval hero John Paul Jones born?

a. Boston, Massachusetts.

b. Annapolis, Maryland.

c. Scotland.

d. The West Indies.

2 Where did the famous battle between the *Bonhomme Richard* and the *Serapis* take place?

a. Off the coast of Virginia.

b. Off the coast of New Jersey.

c. Off the coast of France.

d. Off the coast of England.

3 Why did Jones want to attack the *Serapis*?

a. To seize the cargo of the ships it was guarding.

b. To capture the faster, better-armed ship for the American navy.

c. To prove to the Congress that he should be appointed commander-in-chief of the American naval forces.

d. To bring an end to the Revolutionary War.

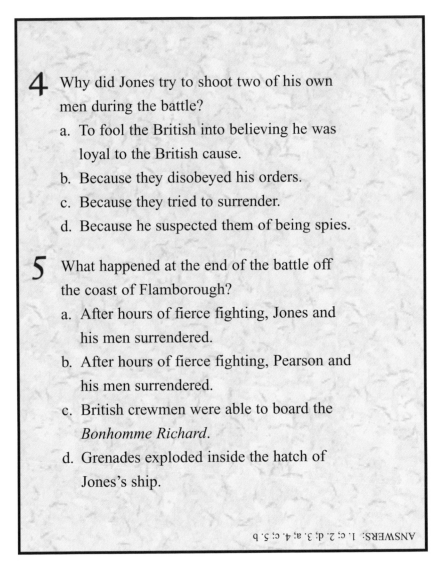

4 Why did Jones try to shoot two of his own men during the battle?

   a. To fool the British into believing he was loyal to the British cause.

   b. Because they disobeyed his orders.

   c. Because they tried to surrender.

   d. Because he suspected them of being spies.

5 What happened at the end of the battle off the coast of Flamborough?

   a. After hours of fierce fighting, Jones and his men surrendered.

   b. After hours of fierce fighting, Pearson and his men surrendered.

   c. British crewmen were able to board the *Bonhomme Richard*.

   d. Grenades exploded inside the hatch of Jones's ship.

ANSWERS: 1. c; 2. d; 3. a; 4. c; 5. b

A
Sailor's
Life

On July 6, 1747, a boy was born in a two-room cottage located along the coast of Scotland. Like his father, his name was John Paul. The baby joined a house already crowded with his parents, one brother, and two sisters.

John's father was a gardener in charge of landscaping Arbigland, a 1,400-acre estate on the Firth of Solway, the body of water that separates England and Scotland. The gardens the elder John Paul designed there were breathtakingly beautiful. Visitors to the estate loved to wander along the carefully built paths lined with colorful flowers, hanging willows, and clear blue ponds. John Paul also oversaw the estate's household staff of about 100 employees. His wife, Jean McDuff, was one of the many house-keepers at Arbigland.

After John Paul's death, his son paid tribute to him with a large grave marker. He had it carved with the words "universally esteemed"[4] to remind those who saw it that his father had been widely respected. But, during his lifetime, the elder John Paul was often angry at his station in life. Despite his hard work, the wealthy owner of Arbigland, William Craik, always treated his gardener as little more than a servant.

Craik's condescending attitude also upset the younger John Paul. Many years later, he wrote, "[Craik's] ungracious conduct to me before I left Scotland I have not yet been able to get the better of. It is true that I bore it seeming unconcern, but Heaven can witness for me, that I suffered the more on that very account."[5]

Despite Craik's behavior, young John Paul had many happy times at Arbigland. As a boy, he often wandered through his father's gardens and down to the shore to watch the rolling waves of the sea. Occasionally, he spied great ships with white linen sails drifting slowly by. The son of William Craik later remembered observing John playing a game with a gang of boys by the seaside. Standing on the edge of the shore, he barked out orders to his friends as they paddled around in rowboats. In his imagination, at least, John was already the commander of a fleet of ships.

In his youth, John attended a parish school. Being from a humble background, John was lucky to get a fairly good education. His childhood lessons in mathematics and geography proved particularly useful in his adult career.

Always ambitious, John longed one day to join the British navy. As he later told Benjamin Franklin, "I had made the art of war at sea in some degree my study and had been fond of the navy, from boyish days up."[6] But John's family did not have the connections he needed to secure a spot in the navy. Instead, he had to settle for a seven-year apprenticeship on a merchant ship.

ABOARD THE *FRIENDSHIP*

In 1760, at the age of 13, John Paul set off on the *Friendship,* on which he worked for the next three years. During that period, he crossed the Atlantic Ocean eight times. On one early voyage, he visited Virginia, one of the 13 colonies of America, which were then controlled by the British government.

As Paul quickly learned, life was hard on a merchant ship. Even the strongest men often got seasick as the ship rocked back and forth. And no one was immune from fear when wild storms blew up and threatened to tear the vessel apart. Even in good weather, the sailors had to endure the ship's unsanitary conditions and foul smells. With no water for bathing, the filthy men and their dirty clothes contributed to the heavy stench.

The ship's owners added to the general misery by doing everything they could to cut costs and increase profits. To save money, they bought cheap food for their crews. Day after day, meals consisted of small portions of rock-hard beef, peas, and biscuits. The only treat the sailors received was a daily ration of rum or beer. Wanting to keep his wits about him, Paul preferred to drink lemonade.

As another cost-saving measure, ship owners hired as few crewmembers as possible. As a result, everyone had to work long hours, often performing backbreaking and dangerous labor day and night. In part to escape this drudgery, Paul was eager to master tasks that required more brains than muscles. With the help of the *Friendship*'s captain, Robert Benson, Paul learned the basics of navigation.

By observing Benson, Paul also learned that a captain was more than just a skilled navigator. He also had to be a manager, able to oversee the work of a team of rough and unruly men. A good captain ran a tight ship, where everyone knew what they had to do and did it well. If a captain failed to keep his crew in line, he ran the risk of his men rebelling and taking over his ship. A mutiny might spell the end not only of a shipping voyage, but of the captain's life as well.

A CAPTAIN AT LAST

In 1764, the owners of the *Friendship* ran into financial trouble and sold the ship. Released from his apprenticeship several years early, Paul looked for another job at sea. He was hired first as a third mate on the *King George* and then as a first mate on the *Two Friends*.

Both vessels were slave ships. They transported captured Africans in chains to slave plantations on the islands in the Caribbean Sea.

Since Jones never wrote about his experience in the slave trade, it is unknown what he thought of it. But by 1767, he had had enough. In Jamaica, Paul left his job on the *Two Friends* and found a captain willing to let him travel on his ship back to Scotland. On the way, the captain and his first mate both fell ill and died. Paul was the only person left on board who knew how to navigate the ship. When he returned it safely to Scotland, the ship's owners were so grateful that they asked him to take the command of a small vessel. Only 21 years old, John Paul was now the captain of his own ship, the *John*.

As a captain, Paul traveled back and forth between Scotland and the West Indies, carrying goods for sale. On his second voyage, he ran into trouble. Paul generally had a calm demeanor, but he sometimes displayed an explosive temper. On this voyage, a crewman named Mungo Maxwell got under his skin. The member of a prominent Scottish family, Maxwell refused to take orders from a mere gardener's son.

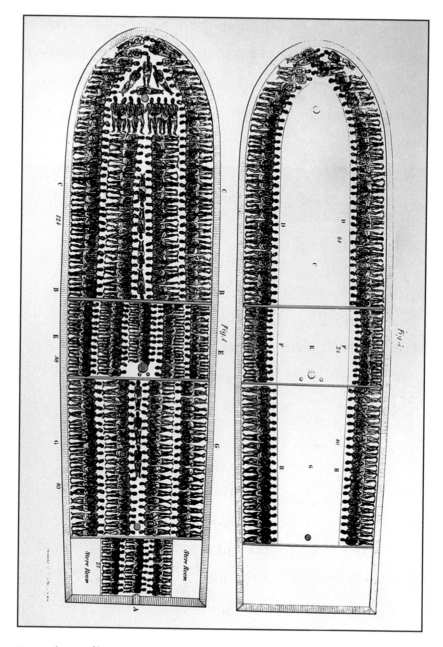

Jones's earliest experiences at sea included serving on two slave ships. The misery and hardship of the slaves is evident from this plan of a slave ship's hold.

Deciding that Maxwell had been disrespectful once too often, Paul ordered that Maxwell be flogged, then a common punishment at sea. The other crewmen stripped Maxwell of his shirt and tied him to a

Freemasonry

In 1770, John Paul joined the Ancient Society of Free and Accepted Masons, better known as the Freemasons. Established first in Scotland, this organization was spreading throughout the world in the eighteenth century. Famous philosophers, politicians, writers, and even kings were proud of their membership in the Freemasons.

The Freemasons created a mythic history of the organization, tracing its origins back to the biblical Adam. They also held secret rituals during their meetings. However, Masonic lodges were mainly gentlemen clubs—places where men could gather with one another and discuss topics of interest. The Freemasons also performed charitable works and promoted new, modern ideas about science and philosophy associated with the movement known as the Enlightenment.

But Paul was drawn to the Freemasons for another reason. In the mid-eighteenth century, it was difficult

post. One then beat his bare back with a cat-o'-nine-tails, made of a piece of wood attached to nine strips of cord. After 12 strokes, Maxwell's flesh was torn to shreds.

for anyone in Europe to rise above the social rank into which he or she was born. Paul had become a respected and moderately wealthy sea captain, but in European society his achievements hardly mattered. Nobles and others of high social status considered him an inferior.

In the Freemasons, however, a successful man like Paul was given the respect he was due. Many of its members were wealthy lawyers and merchants from modest backgrounds. They might be rebuffed in high society, but within a Masonic lodge, they were treated by fellow members as brothers. Freemasonry, therefore, served as a way for men on the rise to meet and gather support from one another. For a sea captain, this aspect of the organization held a special appeal. Nearly everywhere Paul traveled, he could find a Masonic lodge where he would be welcomed with open arms.

When the *John* reached the island of Tobago, Maxwell struck back at Paul. He sued his captain for assault in Admiralty Court, the British court established in Tobago to hear cases involving maritime law. Finding in Paul's favor, the judges declared that Maxwell's punishment had been justified. Relieved to have this trouble behind him, Paul sailed back to Scotland.

When Paul came ashore, however, he was met by a sheriff, who arrested him. Paul then learned that Maxwell had died on his return home, and his influential family was convinced that the flogging was to blame. After posting bail, Paul began gathering evidence for his defense. He obtained a sworn statement from the captain of the ship on which Maxwell had died, saying that an illness, not his wounds, was responsible for his death. With this statement and the court papers from Tobago, Paul persuaded the Scottish court to dismiss the case.

Paul went back to work as the captain of a larger merchant ship, the *Betsy*. He was earning a good living and even managed to save £2,500. He considered using his savings to buy land in Virginia and retire there as a gentleman farmer. But this plan was dashed when another legal case suddenly threatened his livelihood and reputation.

MURDER IN TOBAGO

At the end of 1773, the *Betsy* sailed into port in Tobago. On the trip, much of its cargo of butter and wine had spoiled. Unable to sell his goods, Paul was strapped for cash. Adding to his problems, his men were demanding to be paid so that they could enjoy themselves in Tobago's taverns. Paul refused, saying that they would get their pay after their return to Europe, but not before.

Many of his men started grumbling. The loudest complaints came from a man Paul later called "the Ringleader." He confronted Paul and began cursing at him. Paul tried to calm him down with a gift of some new clothes. The Ringleader was not impressed. He responded to Paul's offer by trying to take over the ship.

Paul ran to his cabin and found his sword. Back on deck, he met the Ringleader, who was now armed with a club. Paul looked around for help. None of his officers were in sight, and the rest of his crew was clearly on the Ringleader's side. According to Paul, the Ringleader rushed at him. Before he could club Paul, the sword sliced through his body. The Ringleader was dead.

Paul believed that this was an obvious case of self-defense that he could quickly clear up in Admiralty Court. But because it was not in session, the case was instead going to be brought before a local court. Since the Ringleader was from Tobago, Paul worried that the jury would sympathize with the victim and find Paul guilty of murder. Weighing the odds, Paul decided that there was only one solution to his predicament: He hired a boat and ran away to the American colonies.

Paul ended up in the town of Fredericksburg on the coast of Virginia. He had hoped to hide at the home of his brother William, who years before had emigrated there and set up shop as a tailor. But once Paul reached Fredericksburg, he discovered that William was dead. Alone and a fugitive from the law, Paul decided to stay in Fredericksburg until the situation in Tobago blew over. No doubt hoping to confuse anyone who might have traced him to Virginia, he changed his name, calling himself John Paul Jones. At 26, with only about £50 in his pocket, he prepared to start a new life in a new place with a new name.

Test Your Knowledge

I   What was Jones's father's profession?

a. He was a sailor.

b. He was a carpenter.

c. He was a silversmith.

d. He was a gardener.

2   While serving as an apprentice on a merchant
ship, what did Jones learn?

a. He learned that the weather was uncertain
and often dangerous.

b. He learned the basics of navigation.

c. He learned that a captain must be a good
manager, keeping his crew busy and disciplined.

d. All of the above.

3   How did Jones become captain of his own ship
at the age of 21?

a. He safely sailed a ship from Jamaica to Scotland
when the captain and first mate became ill.

b. He demonstrated his navigational skills while
sailing from Scotland to Trinidad.

c. He was able to save enough money to purchase
his own ship.

d. He made the trip from Scotland to the West
Indies in record time, proving his skill
and efficiency.

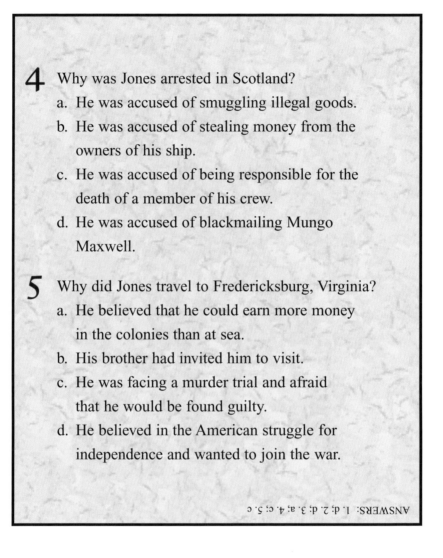

4 Why was Jones arrested in Scotland?

    a. He was accused of smuggling illegal goods.

    b. He was accused of stealing money from the
       owners of his ship.

    c. He was accused of being responsible for the
       death of a member of his crew.

    d. He was accused of blackmailing Mungo
       Maxwell.

5 Why did Jones travel to Fredericksburg, Virginia?

    a. He believed that he could earn more money
       in the colonies than at sea.

    b. His brother had invited him to visit.

    c. He was facing a murder trial and afraid
       that he would be found guilty.

    d. He believed in the American struggle for
       independence and wanted to join the war.

ANSWERS: 1. d; 2. d; 3. a; 4. c; 5. c

Joining the Revolution

While in Fredericksburg, John Paul Jones learned that in one important way, America was no different from Scotland. In both places, a young man had a hard time rising in the world without the help of influential friends or family. Jones found that few people in Virginia society were interested in helping a poor Scotsman with a shady past.

One exception was John K. Read. A doctor and fellow Scotsman, Read became Jones's closest friend in Virginia. Sharing a love of reading, they often met for long, wandering conversations about their favorite books.

It was probably Read who introduced Jones to Dorothea Spottswood Dandridge, a beautiful young woman from one of the colony's most distinguished families. Jones courted her, but the romance quickly fizzled, possibly because her father objected. The penniless and unemployed Jones could hardly have been considered a good catch.

By April 1775, Jones had been in Virginia for about a year. All he had to show for that time was a broken heart and an empty pocket. But then, his fate shifted. A horseman bounded into Fredericksburg, announcing that far to the north in Massachusetts, the American colonists had begun to battle British troops. The American Revolution had begun.

Within days, the streets of Fredericksburg were full of men volunteering to join the fight. Jones, too, caught revolutionary fever. As a Scotsman, he had little love for England, which had long imposed its harsh rule over Scotland. But Jones also had a more personal reason for wanting to fight. During a war, men with talent and ambition could quickly gain recognition and fame. Becoming a war hero could be his path to the highest reaches of American society. By late summer, Jones had left Fredericksburg and headed toward Philadelphia to volunteer for service in the American navy.

There was one major flaw in Jones's plan: The Americans did not yet have a real navy. The Continental Congress, the ruling body of the rebels, appointed a Marine Committee, which set aside money for the construction of 13 frigates. But building these warships would take a while. In the meantime, all the Americans had were a collection of merchant ships and small, single-masted boats known as sloops, which had been outfitted with cannons. This makeshift fleet seemed pathetic in comparison with the British navy. With some 270 warships at its disposal, England was then the greatest naval power in the world.

A NAVAL COMMISSION

Despite the lack of a true navy in which to serve, Jones was eager to become an American naval officer. There were few volunteers with comparable experience. Jones was offered command over the *Providence,* a 70-foot sloop, but he turned down the commission. He was afraid that he did not have enough skill to handle the fast boat, especially since the added weight of cannons made the sloop more liable to tip over. He instead joined the crew of the *Alfred,* one of the Americans' largest ships, as its first lieutenant.

In January 1776, the *Alfred* sailed down the Delaware River and into the Atlantic Ocean. It was part of a fleet of five ships, which also included the *Columbus,* the *Cabot,* the *Andrew Doria,* and the *Providence.* A crowd gathered along the river and cheered as the ships sailed by.

Jones's first weeks in the American navy were full of disappointment. Harsh weather and icy waters made it impossible for the ships to travel far. Many of the men aboard became sick with smallpox, while others grew discouraged and deserted. Jones quickly came to dislike his dim-witted captain, Dudley Saltonstall.

When the ice began to thaw, the fleet finally set out on its first campaign. The navy's commodore, Esek Hopkins, ordered the ships to travel south to New Providence Island in the Bahamas, where the British had built several forts. Hopkins's plan was to attack the

Esek Hopkins served as the commander-in-chief of the makeshift American navy during the Revolutionary War.

forts and make off with their supply of gunpowder, which the American military sorely needed.

From the start, the plan went badly. Sailing too close to the shore, the American ships were spotted by the British, making it impossible to stage a sneak attack. Once on land, the Americans quickly took over one of the forts. While they slept, however, British soldiers hauled away the fort's gunpowder stash. Still, the Americans were able to take back to the colonies nearly 80 cannons and about 16,000 cannonballs and shells.

The American fleet then headed north to the coast of New England. On April 6, 1776, they came upon the *Glasgow,* a huge British warship. Ready for a fight, the crews of the five American ships ran to their battle stations. The first to take on the *Glasgow* was the *Cabot.* Coming under devastating fire, it was quickly disabled. Next, Jones's ship, the *Alfred,* went on the attack. Again, the American ship was no match for the *Glasgow.* A cannonball quickly destroyed the *Alfred*'s steering mechanism, leaving it unable to maneuver into an attack position. The *Glasgow* then took off. The three other American ships followed, but the *Glasgow* was able to escape.

The next day, the American fleet sailed into New London, Connecticut. At first, they were hailed as heroes for taking on the *Glasgow*. But people soon began to question why five American ships had failed to capture one British vessel traveling on its own. Jones sent his report on the battle to Joseph Hewes, a member of the Marine Committee. He defended himself and his men, but took a few shots at Saltonstall for his superior attitude.

Congress investigated the *Glasgow* battle. The only navy man punished was the captain of the *Providence,* who was caught stealing goods from the ship's stores. The navy then again asked Jones to take command of the *Providence.* Eager to get out from under Saltonstall's command, Jones this time took the commission.

ON THE *PROVIDENCE*

In the summer of 1776, while the Continental Congress was debating the draft of the Declaration of Independence, Jones and his crew traveled the Atlantic coast, searching for "prizes." Prizes were British merchant ships loaded with goods. The *Providence* attacked these ships to steal their cargo and, if possible, the ships themselves for the American military.

Jones and his crew traveled the Atlantic searching for "prizes"—
British merchant ships loaded with goods.

Taking a prize gave Captain Jones more than glory. He
also received about ten percent of the worth of the
goods he seized.

While sailing the seas that August, Jones saw a
huge ship in the distance. He thought it might be a
merchant ship, ripe for the taking. As he drew closer,
he realized that it was a warship equipped with 26
guns. The British ship, the *Solebay,* raced to overtake

the *Providence.* With no time to run away, Jones decided on a daring move. He sailed the *Providence* straight toward *Solebay,* but just before it opened fire, he veered his ship to the side. The *Solebay* crew was unable to adjust its sails quickly enough to follow, and the *Providence* escaped. Jones was pleased with his quick thinking. In his report on the incident, he speculated, "our 'Hairbreadth Scape' and the saucy manner of making it must have mortified [the *Solebay*'s captain] not a little."[7]

Jones's good luck continued into the fall. By then, British warships had begun actively hunting for him, but he still managed to evade them. At the same time, Jones kept taking prizes. By early October, he had 16 to his credit. Jones wanted to continue cruising for prizes, but Commodore Hopkins asked him to take on another mission. The British were holding about 100 American prisoners of war, forcing them to work in a coal mine in Nova Scotia, Canada. Jones was charged with rescuing the men before winter set in.

Jones became almost obsessed with saving the prisoners. One simple problem kept him from heading out immediately. The navy had given him three ships—the *Alfred,* the *Providence,* and the *Hampden*—for the mission, but there were not enough sailors to man them. Most able seamen had abandoned the navy to become privateers. With Congress's blessing, privateer ships were sent out to attack British merchant ships. But while Jones and his men received only a fraction of the prizes they took, the privateers were permitted to keep everything they could seize. Jones complained often and loudly about the privateer policy. As long as privateers could earn far more, the American navy would always be inferior.

With only enough men for two ships, Jones headed north on the *Alfred,* with the *Providence* sailing alongside it. The weather was cold and miserable, and his men were cranky. Jones tried to build up morale, reminding them of the importance of their mission. Nevertheless, one morning Jones woke to find the *Providence* was gone. Under the cover of darkness, its crew had slipped away and headed home.

Now on its own, the *Alfred* continued on. In late November, it ran into three ships. Afraid that they were British warships, Jones prepared for battle. But as the *Alfred* charged toward the largest, he saw that it was actually a merchant ship. The prize's cargo included coal from the Nova Scotia mine where the American prisoners were being held. The crew told Jones that the prisoners were no longer there. Rather than face death in the mines, they had agreed to join the British army. Jones was disappointed. His rescue mission ended with no one left to rescue.

Just before Christmas 1776, Jones made his way to Boston. There, to his shock, he discovered that he had been demoted. The navy relieved him of his command of the *Alfred* and reassigned him to the *Providence,* a far smaller ship. The Marine Committee had also made a list of all naval officers, ranked by their seniority. An officer's place on the list determined how fast he would be promoted. Jones was number 18, near the very bottom of the list.

Jones was dismayed and disgusted. Men with no experience at sea ranked higher than he did. Even Saltonstall, who Jones considered completely incompetent, was listed at number four. Jones fired off an angry letter to Hewes, noting, "that such despicable characters should have obtained commissions as commanders in a navy is truly astonishing."[8] Jones had joined the American navy with dreams of honor and glory. But after a year and a half of distinguished service, his adopted country had given him nothing but disrespect.

A Captain and a Poet

Throughout his life, John Paul Jones valued education. Since his formal schooling was meager, as an adult he struggled to improve his mind by reading any book he could find. Jones was particularly drawn to poetry and eventually began writing poems of his own. His poetry, he discovered, helped him move into the ranks of high society. That Jones could both fight furiously at sea and recite gentle verses in the drawing room made him all the more glamorous to his wealthy friends.

Although Jones was hardly a talented poet, he knew how to write verses that highlighted his achievements in the most flattering ways. For instance, in one poem, he presented himself as humble, while at the same time boasting about his war exploits:

> Insulted freedom bled—I felt her cause
> And drew my sword to vindicate her laws
> From principle, and not from vain applause
> I've done my best; self-interest far apart
> And self-reproach a stranger to my heart*

Jones also found poetry a useful tool in courting women. He often recycled his poems by presenting a new lover with a poem that, unknown to her, he had written previously about an earlier conquest. One such love poem was "The Virgin Muse," in which he told his lady all the things that he would do for her if he were "the king of the sea":

> Were I, Paul Jones, dear maid, "the king of sea,"
> I find such merit in they virgin song,
> A coral crown with bays I'd give to thee,
> A car which on the waves should smoothly glide along.**

Jones's experiments in verse also led him into an interesting friendship. While in Boston in 1777, Jones met Phillis Wheatley, a former slave who had become a celebrated poet. He proudly sent a selection of his verses to Wheatley, addressing them to "the African favorite of the Nine [Muses] and Apollo."***

---

* Evan Thomas, *John Paul Jones: Sailor, Hero, Father of the American Navy* (New York: Simon and Schuster, 2003), 219.

** Samuel Eliot Morison, *John Paul Jones: A Sailor's Biography* (Boston: Little, Brown and Company, 1959), 261.

*** Ibid., 113.

Test Your Knowledge

I Why did Jones join the colonists in their fight for independence from Britain?

    a. He believed that it was a good way to gain fame and become accepted in American society.

    b. Dorothea Dandridge's father encouraged him to enlist.

    c. He was impressed by the American navy and wanted to captain one of their battleships.

    d. He was inspired by the stirring speeches of the Virginia delegates to the Continental Congress.

2 Why did Jones initially turn down the command of the *Providence*?

    a. He believed that the *Alfred* was a much better ship.

    b. He wanted the experience of serving under Dudley Saltonstall.

    c. He did not think he had the necessary skill to captain a fast sloop.

    d. He was concerned that the *Providence* was not seaworthy.

3 Why was Jones so eager to capture "prizes" along the Atlantic coast?

    a. The cargo could be given to the American cause.

    b. Jones received a percentage of the goods he seized.

    c. The ships could be used by the American military.

    d. All of the above.

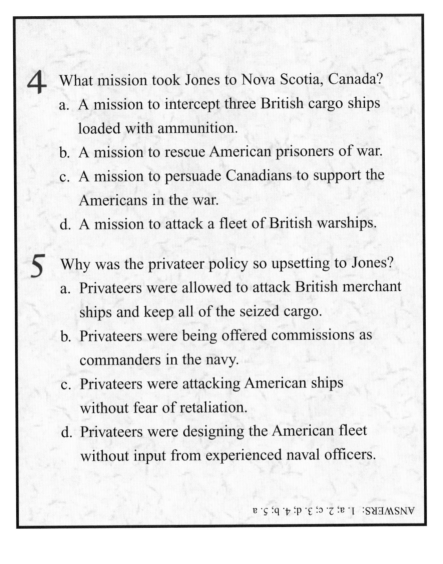

4 What mission took Jones to Nova Scotia, Canada?

a. A mission to intercept three British cargo ships loaded with ammunition.

b. A mission to rescue American prisoners of war.

c. A mission to persuade Canadians to support the Americans in the war.

d. A mission to attack a fleet of British warships.

5 Why was the privateer policy so upsetting to Jones?

a. Privateers were allowed to attack British merchant ships and keep all of the seized cargo.

b. Privateers were being offered commissions as commanders in the navy.

c. Privateers were attacking American ships without fear of retaliation.

d. Privateers were designing the American fleet without input from experienced naval officers.

ANSWERS: 1. a; 2. c; 3. d; 4. b; 5. a

OUR RIGHTS AND OUR LIBERTIES

On the *Ranger*

In the first months of 1777, John Paul Jones was desperate to return to sea. He knew that he was one of America's best naval men and wanted the chance to prove it. Jones wrote letters to Congress, asking first for a fleet to command and then for just one decent vessel to captain.

By March, his patience was gone. He left Boston for Philadelphia, where the Continental Congress was meeting. He argued his case to John Hancock, the president of the Congress. Hancock was encouraging, but still Jones did not receive a commission.

Frustrated and disappointed, Jones returned to Boston. Finally, in May, he received the letter for which he had been hoping. In it, Congress told him to go to Portsmouth, New Hampshire. From there, he would take a French ship, the *Amphitrite,* to France, where a fine frigate would be waiting for him, ready for his command.

Jones rushed to Portsmouth only to find that the captain of the *Amphitrite* would not let him board. Congress demanded that the *Amphitrite*'s captain share command with Jones on the way to Europe—a condition the captain refused to comply with. The *Amphitrite* sailed to Europe without Jones.

Still, there was some good news for Jones in Portsmouth. Congress ultimately arranged for him to get his own ship, a brand-new sloop called the *Ranger,* to sail to France. Jones immediately set about hiring a crew for the *Ranger.* He tacked up posters throughout the port town, recruiting "ALL GENTLEMEN SEAMEN and able-bodied LANDSMEN who have a mind to distinguish themselves in the GLORIOUS CAUSE of their country."[9] Despite his rousing advertisement, he had trouble finding sailors willing to sign up, and those who did were less than ideal. As Jones soon found out, they were far less interested in serving the glorious cause than in making a little money by capturing prizes.

After a fairly uneventful trip, the *Ranger* arrived in the French port of Nantes on December 2, 1777. Jones then headed to Paris by carriage, leaving behind his untested crew and his ship. Once in the French capital, he went to the Hotel Valentinois, which was serving as the American headquarters in Paris. There, he met with Benjamin Franklin, Silas Deane, and Arthur Lee—the members of the American commission charged with persuading France to become an official ally in the War for Independence.

France was already interested in helping the Americans. After all, they were fighting England, France's longtime enemy. But the French were still not convinced that the Americans could win the revolution, although there was one new development that was encouraging. About two months before Jones arrived

In Paris, Jones met with Benjamin Franklin, who was part of the American delegation charged with persuading the French to support the Americans in their fight for independence.

in Paris, the British army under John Burgoyne had surrendered to American forces at Saratoga.

Jones wanted to do his part to get French support. He excitedly told the commissioners of his plans and strategies for harassing English towns and ships. But, at least at first, the commissioners only had bad news for Jones. The frigate he had been promised, a ship called the *Indien,* was being built in Holland. Under pressure from the British, the Dutch had decided not to sell the *Indien* to France after all. For the time being, Jones was stuck with commanding the far less impressive *Ranger.*

While meeting with the commissioners, Jones got a brief taste of Parisian high society. Very popular with the French, Franklin liked to hold lavish dinners for his many friends. Although Jones spoke little French, he could sense the exotic and exciting social rituals of the wealthy. Married men and women openly flirted. It was an elegant, captivating world, far removed from the challenges of life at sea.

PLAN OF ATTACK

While Jones enjoyed himself in Paris, his crew was falling apart. By the time he returned to the *Ranger* in late January 1778, he found that many of his men had deserted. Those left were annoyed that their captain had been away so long. They wanted to get out to sea to collect prizes.

But Jones had something else in mind for the *Ranger.* He knew that the British forces in America had been burning and looting colonial towns. Jones decided it was therefore fair for him to do the same to towns along the coast of England.

Jones's ambitious plans included a campaign to burn and loot English port cities and a plot to kidnap the Earl of Selkirk.

Jones's first target was the town of Whitehaven. He knew it well. It was from this British port that he had first sailed as an apprentice when he was only 13 years old. Jones also devised a plot to kidnap the Earl of Selkirk, who lived nearby. The earl had been a frequent visitor to Arbigland, the estate on which Jones had been raised. Jones said that he wanted to kidnap the earl and ransom him for American prisoners held by the British. But, privately, Jones must have relished the chance to humiliate a man who, during Jones's youth, had treated his father with disrespect.

Heading toward Whitehaven, Jones discovered that his men were not thrilled by his plan. They did not want to fight the English. If they were not going to take prizes, they wanted to go home. Jones had only one friend among his officers, a man named Jean Meijer. Meijer told Jones that the crew was ready to mutiny. According to their plot, the *Ranger*'s master, David Cullam, would attack Jones, setting off the takeover. With Meijer's warning, Jones readied himself to respond. When Cullam rushed for him, he swiftly pulled out his pistol and put it to the master's head. The rest of the crew backed away, and the mutinous grumbling died down.

Just as the *Ranger* reached the English coast, Jones spied the *Hussar,* a small British ship looking for smugglers. Here, Jones thought, was a prize worth taking. He raised a British flag above the *Ranger,* hoping to fool the *Hussar*'s captain. But when the two ships came close to each other, Jones gave up the ploy. The shooting started, and the *Hussar* made a run for it and escaped. Even worse, Jones knew that the captain would soon alert coastal towns of the *Ranger*'s presence. He had little time left to make a sneak attack on Whitehaven.

As the *Ranger* raced toward the town, Jones learned that another British ship, the *Drake,* was nearby. He decided to try to surprise its crew as they slept. The *Ranger* crept up alongside the *Drake,* intending to drop anchor so that Jones's men could board the British vessel. But his men failed to drop the anchor fast enough, and the *Ranger* sailed on. Again, a valuable prize was lost.

Jones returned his focus to Whitehaven. But when he asked for volunteers to rush into the town, he could not find any among his crew. Even his first and second lieutenants, Thomas Simpson and Elijah Hall, refused, claiming that they were too tired.

Finally, Jones was able to shame about 30 seaman into joining his attack on Whitehaven. In the middle of the night, they boarded several rowboats. Just before dawn, they reached the shore. With a handful of men, Jones crept into the town's fort and disabled

Lady Selkirk's Silver

In April 1778, John Paul Jones was determined to kidnap the Earl of Selkirk, a Scottish nobleman. He assumed that Selkirk's family would offer him a large amount of money as a ransom. But Jones had already decided to reject any sum, no matter how large, and planned to release Selkirk only in exchange for the release of American prisoners held in British jails. The plan would allow Jones to present himself to the world in a way that pleased him. He would show that he was a man of character, motivated not by money, but by honor.

Despite his planning, however, the kidnapping plot fell apart. He and a group of his men stormed the earl's estate only to find that Selkirk was not at home. Jones wanted to leave, but his men refused to go away empty-handed.

Jones was in a bind. If he let the men attack the mansion, they might tear the house apart, or attack Selkirk's family. But if he tried to stop them, they might attack

its cannons, leaving the townspeople largely defenseless.

When Jones returned to Whitehaven's pier, he found that the rest of his men were drunk. He had told them to set fire to the ships there. Instead, they had broken

him, then destroy the mansion anyway. Jones told his men that they could go into the house, but that they could take nothing more than the family's silver set. Amazingly, the men followed these orders. They approached the house, politely asked the earl's wife for her silver, drank some wine, and left.

Still, the incident weighed on Jones. He did not want to be thought a thief, nor did he want to be linked to the behavior of his men. Once he returned to France, he wrote Lady Selkirk a note of apology. Its language was oddly flowery, clearly designed to convince her that he, unlike his crew, was a man "of fine feelings and of real sensibility."* Jones also vowed to return the stolen goods. Although it took more than seven years and a great deal of money, Jones hunted down a plate and teapot and returned them to Lady Selkirk.

* Evan Thomas, *John Paul Jones: Sailor, Hero, Father of the American Navy* (New York: Simon and Schuster, 2003), 137.

into a tavern. When Jones again ordered them to burn the vessels, his men explained that their lanterns had gone out. Disgusted, Jones broke into a house, stole a lighted candle, and threw it into a ship. The vessel went up in flames, but the fire did not spread to the other ships as Jones hoped. Seeing the blaze, the townspeople ran to the shore. Jones and his men scrambled into their rowboats and escaped to the *Ranger.*

TAKING THE *DRAKE*

Without a moment of rest, Jones decided to move to the next part of his plan. By about 11 o'clock in the morning, the *Ranger* reached the village of Kirkcudbright, the home of the Earl of Selkirk. With a dozen men, Jones took a rowboat ashore and climbed a path to the earl's mansion. Along the way, he ran into the gardener, who told him that the earl was away. Jones's men stole some silver from Selkirk's wife, but left without their intended prize—the earl himself.

Jones's expedition had hardly been a success. He could not bear to return to France until he had had a real victory. To save face, he decided to hunt down the *Drake* and go to battle with the British vessel. Jones found the *Drake* off the coast of northern Ireland. Using his old trick, he raised a British flag. This time it worked. An officer and a few crewmen from the *Drake* sailed out to welcome the *Ranger.* Jones invited them on board, then informed them that they were prisoners of war.

Jones ordered his men to beat to quarters. For more than an hour, the two ships battled. They were fairly evenly matched, although the *Drake* had a larger, much more disciplined crew. During the fighting, the Americans managed to kill the British captain and first officer. After an intense battering, the *Drake*'s master finally called out, "Quarters!" Jones was the victor, the first American captain ever to defeat a British ship.

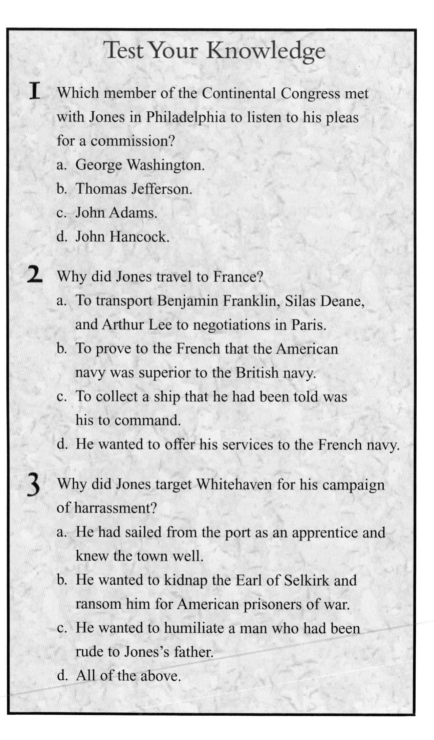

Test Your Knowledge

I Which member of the Continental Congress met with Jones in Philadelphia to listen to his pleas for a commission?

a. George Washington.

b. Thomas Jefferson.

c. John Adams.

d. John Hancock.

2 Why did Jones travel to France?

a. To transport Benjamin Franklin, Silas Deane, and Arthur Lee to negotiations in Paris.

b. To prove to the French that the American navy was superior to the British navy.

c. To collect a ship that he had been told was his to command.

d. He wanted to offer his services to the French navy.

3 Why did Jones target Whitehaven for his campaign of harrassment?

a. He had sailed from the port as an apprentice and knew the town well.

b. He wanted to kidnap the Earl of Selkirk and ransom him for American prisoners of war.

c. He wanted to humiliate a man who had been rude to Jones's father.

d. All of the above.

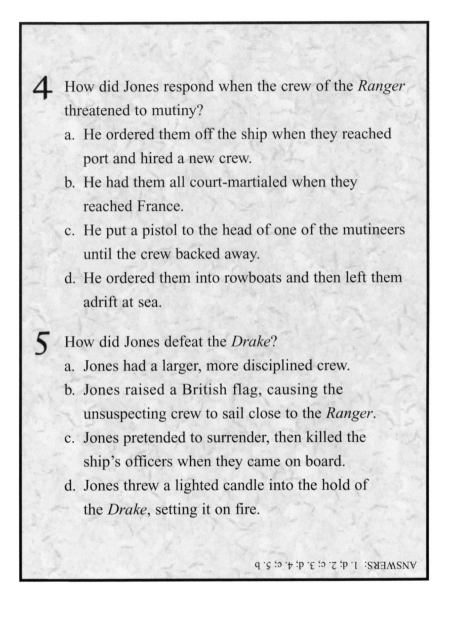

4 How did Jones respond when the crew of the *Ranger* threatened to mutiny?

   a. He ordered them off the ship when they reached port and hired a new crew.

   b. He had them all court-martialed when they reached France.

   c. He put a pistol to the head of one of the mutineers until the crew backed away.

   d. He ordered them into rowboats and then left them adrift at sea.

5 How did Jones defeat the *Drake*?

   a. Jones had a larger, more disciplined crew.

   b. Jones raised a British flag, causing the unsuspecting crew to sail close to the *Ranger*.

   c. Jones pretended to surrender, then killed the ship's officers when they came on board.

   d. Jones threw a lighted candle into the hold of the *Drake*, setting it on fire.

ANSWERS: 1. d; 2. c; 3. d; 4. c; 5. b

Itching
for a Fight

Minutes after the crew of the *Drake* surrendered, Jones sent a boatload of men to take possession of the prize. They spent the night patching up the British ship, and by morning's light, both the *Drake* and the *Ranger* were heading up the coast of Ireland toward France. Knowing that

British warships would be sent after him, Jones was eager to make a quick getaway.

On the trip to France, Jones came upon a Swedish merchant ship. Unable to resist taking another prize, he steered the *Ranger* toward her. But before he reached the Swedish vessel, he realized that the *Drake* had disappeared. Jones gave up his prize to chase after the missing ship. About a day later, the *Ranger* overtook the *Drake,* which was commanded by Jones's deceitful first lieutenant Thomas Simpson. Jones had had enough of Simpson's insubordination. He promptly arrested the officer for disobeying his orders to stay close to the *Ranger.*

On May 7, 1778, both ships arrived safely at the French port city of Brent. At about the same time, news of Jones's recent exploits reached Paris. In a sense, his expedition was not much of a success. He had taken the *Drake,* but during his attack on Whitehaven he had destroyed only a single ship. And his attempted kidnapping of Lord Selkirk was a complete disaster. However, Jones had done something extraordinary: He had forced English citizens to think carefully about the personal costs and consequences of the American

The Pirate Paul Jones

John Paul Jones joined the American navy in part to win fame as a war hero. But after his attack on the town of Whitehaven, he earned a very different reputation among the people of England. Calling him the "Pirate Paul Jones," they considered him the greatest villain among the American rebels.

Parents told their children frightening tales about Jones. Books pictured him as a crude thief and murderer, determined to loot and kill innocent families. Newspapers recounted fanciful stories about how Jones shot his own men when they disobeyed his orders and how, as a child, he beat his teacher nearly to death. Although Jones was always careful about his dress, many accounts depicted him in the rough clothing of an outlaw. One said that he "dressed in a short jacket and long trousers with about twelve charged pistols slung in a belt around his middle and a cutlass [sword] in his hand."*

There were even popular tavern songs dedicated to demonizing Jones. One drew on Jones's thwarted plot to kidnap the Earl of Selkirk:

> You have heard o' Paul Jones?
> Have you not? Have you not?

And you've heard o' Paul Jones?
Have you not?

A rogue and a vagabond;
Is he not? Is he not?

He came to Selkirk-ha'
Did he not? Did he not?

And stole the rings and the jewels a',
Did he not? Did he not?

Robbed the plate and jewels a'
Which did his conscience gall,
Did it not?**

The British navy, embarrassed by Jones's victories, was happy to spread stories that depicted him as a fiend. At least in one way, however, this campaign backfired. The more that the British heard about the fearsome Jones, the more they wondered whether the war against the American colonies was worth fighting. Spreading fear of Jones also helped to spread antiwar sentiments.

* Evan Thomas, *John Paul Jones: Sailor, Hero, Father of the American Navy* (New York: Simon and Schuster, 2003), 200.

** Samuel Eliot Morison, *John Paul Jones: A Sailor's Biography* (Boston: Little, Brown and Company, 1959), 163.

Revolution. As Jones himself wrote, "What was done
. . . is sufficient to show that not all their boasted navy
can protect their own coasts and that the scenes of
distress which they have occasioned in America may
soon be brought home to their own doors."[10]

Given the panic Jones had spread throughout
England, he reasonably expected to receive a hero's
welcome in France. But for weeks he heard nothing
from the American commissioners in Paris. Jones
grumbled and stewed, as he always did when he felt
unappreciated. Finally, Benjamin Franklin wrote him a
note of congratulations, which helped soothe Jones's
hurt feelings. Even better, Franklin sent word in early
June that Jones would get command over the *Indien,*
the brand-new Dutch frigate he had been promised the
year before.

Heartened, Jones left for Paris to meet with Antoine
de Sartine, the official in charge of the French navy.
Jones outlined for him an ambitious plot to attack fish-
ing towns in Scotland and Ireland and to destroy the
coal shipping industry centered in Newcastle. The
Newcastle attack would prevent coal from reaching
London, ensuring a cold and difficult winter in the
English capital. The French official seemed supportive

of Jones's plans and even hinted that he would be able to get Jones a small fleet.

While outlining his schemes, Jones also enjoyed Paris society. With their shared interest in lavish dinners and elegant parties, Jones and Franklin became closer. Jones, however, grew suspicious of the other two commissioners, Arthur Lee and John Adams (who had replaced Silas Deane). These commissioners were upset by Jones's charges against Simpson and wanted the officer freed from jail so that he could take the *Ranger* back to America. Under pressure, Jones decided to release Simpson, though he continued to insist that the lieutenant had behaved terribly.

Soon, Jones faced even bigger troubles. Much to his disappointment, he lost the *Indien* when Holland again refused to sell it to France. It also became clear that Sartine's promises to give him additional ships would not be kept. Returning to Brest, Jones increasingly felt out of favor with both the American commissioners and the French naval officials. He suspected that Simpson and the crew of the *Ranger* had been spreading rumors about him. With no ship, he had nothing to do but brood over his mistreatment. Unable to sleep for days at a time, Jones was close to mental collapse.

But even at his most desperate moments, Jones did not consider quitting his commission, although he surely could have found fortune and fame as a privateer. Instead, Jones stayed fiercely loyal to the American navy and even predicted, against all evidence, that it would one day be the greatest on the globe. Writing to a friend in November 1778, he claimed, "Tho' I am no prophet . . . [the American navy will become] the first Navy within a much shorter space of time than is generally imagined. When the enemies' land force is once conquered and expelled from the continent, our Marine will rise as if by enchantment and become, within the memory of persons now living, the wonder and envy of the world."[11]

THE *BONHOMME RICHARD*

In early December, Jones at last received some encouraging news. He learned that an old merchant ship, the *Duc de Duras,* was up for sale. Although it was battered from numerous trips to China, Jones thought it had potential. He especially liked its luxurious cabin, decorated with intricate wood carvings and gold. Jones headed off to Paris, where he persuaded Sartine to buy the ship for him. Jones then renamed it the *Bonhomme*

Jones relished each naval engagement, and predicted that the American navy would one day become the greatest in the world.

Richard, a tribute to Franklin's famous book *Poor Richard's Almanac* (known in France by the title *Les Maximes du Bonhomme Richard*).

The next few months were busy. Jones struggled to turn the *Bonhomme Richard* into a functional warship and to recruit a crew of hundreds. In April 1779, he received a letter from the French, ordering him to meet

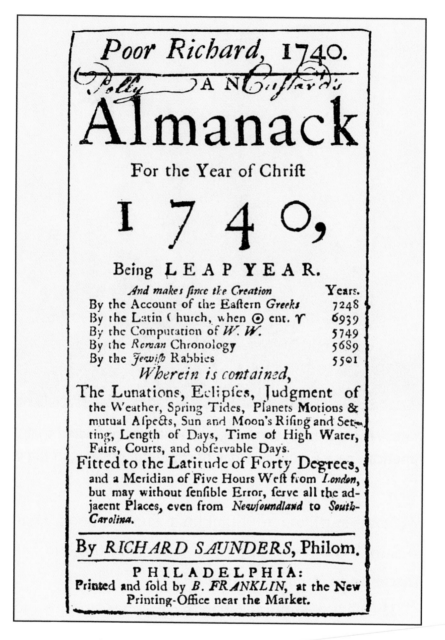

Jones named his ship *Bonhomme Richard* as a tribute to Benjamin Franklin, using part of the French translation for Franklin's *Poor Richard's Almanac*.

with the Marquis de Lafayette, a young Frenchman who was serving as a general in the American army. Lafayette, in consultation with Franklin and Sartine, had proposed land attacks on several British towns. Remembering Jones's similar plans, the French suggested that Lafayette and Jones work together on a joint land-and-sea mission. Both men were enthusiastic about the plan. However, the French king abruptly changed his mind about the campaign and aborted the mission.

Jones still had the *Bonhomme Richard.* In addition, the French had finally agreed to provide him with a small squadron that included four other ships—the *Alliance,* the *Pallas,* the *Cerf,* and the *Vengeance.* Jones, however, continued to have trouble assembling and controlling his crew. Learning that a few men were planning a mutiny, Jones had the leader flogged almost to death.

Another threat to Jones's command came from Pierre Landais, a Frenchman in charge of the *Alliance.* Landais was widely considered one of the worst captains in the American army. He was indecisive, jealous, and incompetent. Even before the fleet had set out on its first mission, the first lieutenant of the *Bonhomme Richard* accidentally rammed straight into the *Alliance*. When Landais saw the *Bonhomme Richard* headed for his ship, he incorrectly assumed its crew was mutinying. Instead of simply changing the *Alliance*'s course, he ran down to his cabin to grab a pistol with which to protect himself.

Jones's men had to stop to repair the two ships. Finally, in mid-August of 1779, the squadron was ready to leave France for the coast of England. It had been nearly a year and half since Jones's encounter with *Drake*. Even with his motley crew and his ill-fitted ship, he was more than ready for a fight.

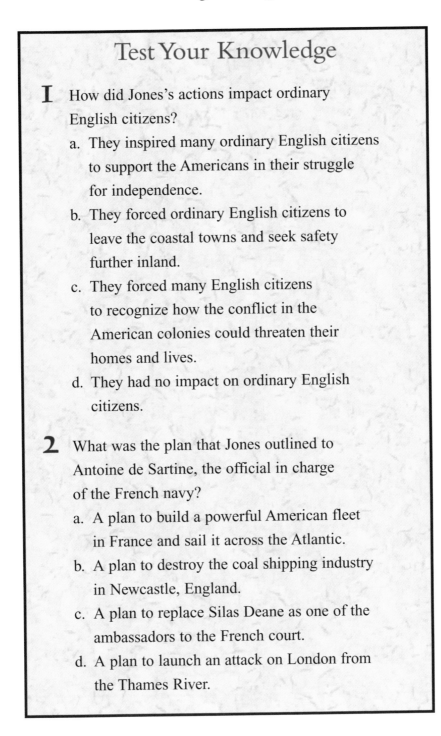

Test Your Knowledge

1 How did Jones's actions impact ordinary English citizens?

    a. They inspired many ordinary English citizens to support the Americans in their struggle for independence.

    b. They forced ordinary English citizens to leave the coastal towns and seek safety further inland.

    c. They forced many English citizens to recognize how the conflict in the American colonies could threaten their homes and lives.

    d. They had no impact on ordinary English citizens.

2 What was the plan that Jones outlined to Antoine de Sartine, the official in charge of the French navy?

    a. A plan to build a powerful American fleet in France and sail it across the Atlantic.

    b. A plan to destroy the coal shipping industry in Newcastle, England.

    c. A plan to replace Silas Deane as one of the ambassadors to the French court.

    d. A plan to launch an attack on London from the Thames River.

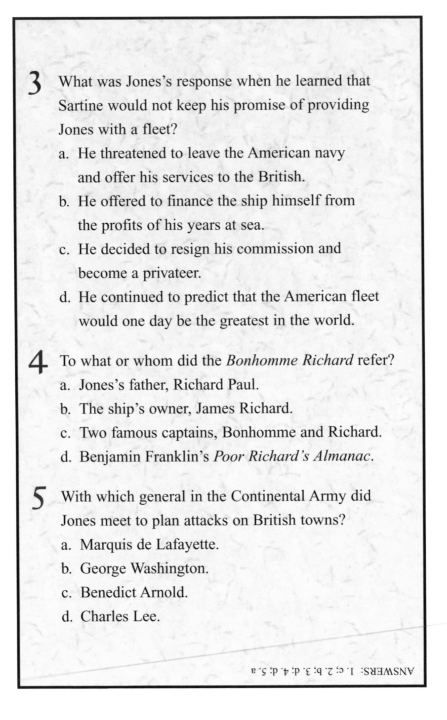

3 What was Jones's response when he learned that Sartine would not keep his promise of providing Jones with a fleet?

a. He threatened to leave the American navy and offer his services to the British.

b. He offered to finance the ship himself from the profits of his years at sea.

c. He decided to resign his commission and become a privateer.

d. He continued to predict that the American fleet would one day be the greatest in the world.

4 To what or whom did the *Bonhomme Richard* refer?

a. Jones's father, Richard Paul.

b. The ship's owner, James Richard.

c. Two famous captains, Bonhomme and Richard.

d. Benjamin Franklin's *Poor Richard's Almanac*.

5 With which general in the Continental Army did Jones meet to plan attacks on British towns?

a. Marquis de Lafayette.

b. George Washington.

c. Benedict Arnold.

d. Charles Lee.

ANSWERS: 1. c; 2. b; 3. d; 4. d; 5. a

6

A Naval Hero

By August 1779, John Paul Jones was eager for battle. The French navy, however, had something else in mind for his five-ship squadron. It ordered him to harass merchant ships along the British coast. These attacks were supposed to distract the British navy, deflecting attention from France's real battle plan. Its navy had assembled a huge fleet of French and Spanish ships to fight British warships for control over the English Channel, the body of water separating England and France.

Jones was not happy being pushed to the sidelines. He ignored the new orders, pretending to believe that he was still bound to earlier orders from Sartine that essentially gave him the freedom to do whatever he wished. Jones decided to lead his ships in a circle around the British Isles, guessing that they could claim a few prizes along the way. But his main goal was to take a British coastal town hostage.

For the citizens of England, Jones's plan was their worst nightmare. Along the coast, residents were already terrified of an attack from the sea. They scrambled to assemble militias to fight back. Wild rumors about what might happen spread from town to town, especially after the French and Spanish fleet was spotted near the shore.

But, unknown to the panicked British, the great fleet was in trouble. Disease was spreading through the crews of the ships. With so many men weakened by illness, the French navy gave up their grand scheme to take on the British navy.

Jones still had his big plans, although his squadron was shrinking. Early in their mission, a gale blew up, and one of his ships, the *Cerf,* disappeared. Soon after, Jones faced another type of storm, when Pierre Landais, captain of the *Alliance,* began disobeying him. Jones confronted Landais, and in the course of their argument, Jones called him a liar. Landais became upset and challenged Jones to a duel. Jones calmed the situation, but thereafter he and Landais considered each other enemies. Landais completely ignored Jones's commands and sailed the *Alliance* wherever he wanted.

Having lost the *Cerf* and the *Alliance,* Jones was left with his ship, the *Bonhomme Richard,* and two others, the *Pallas* and *Vengeance.* Calling together the captains of those two ships, Jones explained that he wanted the squadron to head to Leith, a port town near Edinborough, Scotland. According to Jones's plan, they would take the town hostage and threaten to set it on fire unless the British released American prisoners of war. Neither of Jones's captains was excited by the plot. To get their cooperation, Jones agreed to ransom the town not for prisoners, but for a cash prize, of which the captains would get a healthy cut.

Even with the help of the two captains, Jones's plot fell apart. He planned a raid on the town at dawn, but a storm caught him unawares. It battered his ships, severely damaging the *Bonhomme Richard.* Jones's attack on Leith was over before it could begin.

Jones wanted to raid another town, this time setting his sights on Newcastle. However, his captains refused. English warships were hunting for them, and if they appeared close to the shore, the captains were sure that they would all be captured and hanged.

A LONG-AWAITED VICTORY

Jones was despondent. He had been at sea for weeks and had only a few prizes to show for it. And his time was running out. The French navy wanted him in Amsterdam, the capital of Holland, in early October to escort some French merchant ships on their trip home. Jones feared that his chance for a grand sea battle had passed.

It was on the way to France that Jones came upon the *Serapis* on September 23, 1779. His battle with this English warship became the stuff of legends. And Jones's victory assured his reputation as the American navy's most talented and courageous captain.

Jones's battle with the *Serapis* made him a legend and assured him a reputation as the American navy's most courageous captain.

Although the battle made Jones a hero, it took a heavy toll on his crew. About half the men aboard the *Bonhomme Richard* were killed or wounded. The casualty rate aboard the *Serapis* was about the same. The survivors on the British warship helped Jones and his men patch up the two ships in the battle's aftermath. Jones desperately wanted to make the *Bonhomme Richard* seaworthy again, but it was no use. Jones ordered his men to abandon the ship and board the

Serapis. From the repaired British ship, Jones watched as the *Bonhomme Richard* sank into the deep sea.

Once the *Bonhomme Richard* was gone, Jones set off for Holland. Some eight English warships were hunting for him. For more than a week, the *Serapis* eluded the ships, finally reaching Texel Island off the Dutch coast on October 3. Onboard was valuable cargo—about 500 British prisoners who Jones hoped to exchange for Americans in British jails.

Jones wanted to monitor the prisoner exchange personally. After three days, he left for Amsterdam to oversee the negotiations. News of his exploits had already reached the Dutch city, and hundreds came out to greet him. For a man who constantly craved recognition, the reception must have been gratifying. But Jones handled the attention with grace, belying all the press accounts that described him as a vulgar pirate. As one correspondent noted, "[H]e is a very different man from what he is generally represented; good sense, a genteel address, and a very good, though small person." [12]

Jones enjoyed being the toast of Amsterdam. He attended many parties and dinners in his honor and, after weeks at sea, welcomed the chance to romance beautiful young women in the city's highest social circles. But soon he felt pressure to return to Texel. His men, biding their time there on the *Serapis,* were not happy. The weather was cold and wet, and many of the wounded were not being treated. Jones tried to soothe their anger by appealing to the French ambassador in Holland for pay, food, and clothing for his crew.

At the same time, Jones had to deal with the Dutch authorities, who were under pressure by the British to arrest him. The Dutch instead sent a squadron of warships to Texel to force him leave. To placate the Dutch, the French took control of all of Jones's ships, except the *Alliance.* Annoyed at the Dutch, the French, and his crew, Jones finally set out on the *Alliance* in late December. Dodging British warships the entire way, he arrived at L'Orient in France on February 10. Exhausted and ill, Jones wrote a friend that he was considering retiring from the American navy.

Benjamin Franklin, though, had other plans for Jones. He wanted the captain to take the *Alliance,* loaded with desperately needed supplies for the army, to America. Before leaving, Jones was determined to get the money he and his men were owed for the prizes they had seized. In April, he headed off for Paris, leaving the *Alliance* docked at L'Orient.

Romance with a Countess

While in Paris during the spring of 1780, John Paul Jones wooed many women. Always immaculately dressed in his captain's uniform, he surprised them with his gentle manner and quiet speaking voice. Often, Jones recited his own poems to the women he pursued, insisting to each that she alone was his inspiration.

Among his most difficult conquests was Charlotte-Marguerite de Bourbon, Madame La Comtesse de Lowendahl. She was a young and beautiful noblewoman married to a French brigadier general. Jones was immediately smitten with the countess. She, too, showed interest in Jones, though perhaps because she hoped for Jones's help in furthering her husband's military career.

During their flirtation, the countess painted a miniature portrait of Jones. He treasured it as a token of love. After leaving Paris, Jones sent her an affectionate letter, in which he wrote, "You have made me in love with my own picture because you have condescended to draw it."* With the letter, he enclosed a lock of his hair, but he said that he would send her his heart if it would make her happy.

The intensity of Jones's feelings may have alarmed the countess. She also might have cooled to him after a friend of hers, Caroline Edes, wrote about the countess's romance with Jones in an English newspaper. Edes explained that Jones was "greatly admired here especially by the ladies, who are wild with love for him, but he adores Lady———who has honored him with every mark of politeness and attention."[**] Even though, she did not use the countess's name, it was clear to everyone in French society who was the subject of Edes's allusion. Among the countess's friends, having a discreet affair was acceptable but advertising it in such a public way was not.

To fight off the gossips, the countess wrote back to Jones, pretending that she did not understand why he had sent her such a heartfelt letter. She, of course, could not return his feelings, "without deceiving a gentleman with whom I live, and I am incapable of doing that."[***] Though annoyed, Jones took her rejection in stride. After all, there were plenty of other young beauties who would welcome the attentions of a dashing war hero.

[*] Evan Thomas, *John Paul Jones: Sailor, Hero, Father of the American Navy* (New York: Simon and Schuster, 2003), 222.

[**] Samuel Eliot Morison, *John Paul Jones: A Sailor's Biography* (Boston: Little, Brown and Company, 1959), 280.

[***] Thomas, *John Paul Jones,* 223.

Jones undoubtedly had an ulterior motive for traveling to the French capital. After his reception in Amsterdam, he expected to be greeted as a celebrity in Paris. He was not disappointed. The French nobility embraced the notorious captain. Night after night, he was invited to the opera, to the theater, and to lavish parties. Jones was supposed to remain in Paris for a few days. But, unable to tear himself away from the city's nightlife, he ended up staying six weeks. During that time, he received many honors. Jones sat for the famous sculptor Houdin, who made a bust of his image. He was invited to join the Nine Sisters, the most distinguished Masonic lodge in the world. And he visited with King Louis XVI, who presented him with an engraved sword and made him a chevalier, the French equivalent of a knight.

FIGHTING FOR THE *ALLIANCE*

Jones did not realize that, while he was enjoying Paris, his old rival Landais was brewing trouble in L'Orient. He persuaded the officers and crew of the *Alliance* to turn on Jones. Franklin found out that Landais was plotting to take over the ship and wrote Jones to warn him. Jones rushed back to L'Orient, but he was too late.

The French king Louis XVI was so impressed by Jones's exploits that he presented the captain with an engraved sword and made him a chevalier, the French equivalent of a knight.

Landais had taken command. The few crewmen who had remained loyal to Jones were taken below deck and placed in chains.

Jones was stunned. He rushed back to Paris to plea for help. A few days later, he was in L'Orient, waving orders from the king that stated that Jones was the rightful captain of the *Alliance.* Landais responded by sailing the *Alliance* into the Atlantic, bound for America. Oddly, even though the French navy had warships poised to chase down the runaway vessel, Jones did nothing to stop Landais. Perhaps Jones was so tired of dealing with him that he was relieved to see him go.

When Franklin learned what had happened, he turned on Jones. He could not believe that Jones would let the *Alliance* get away, since the ship was needed to carry goods to the army. When the French gave Jones a new ship, the *Ariel,* Franklin wrote an angry letter to the captain, insisting he leave for America as soon as possible. Even so, Jones dallied for months, hoping to gain more support from the French for his military schemes and to secure the long-promised prize money. Finally, in early September, he agreed to leave. Jones threw his own going-away party on the *Ariel.* The night was filled with fine food, lilting music, and fireworks.

At the end of the festivities, Jones staged a recreation of his battle with the *Serapis,* with his men running around shooting cannons and waving swords. Jones wanted to make sure that his French friends did not forget his most heroic moment.

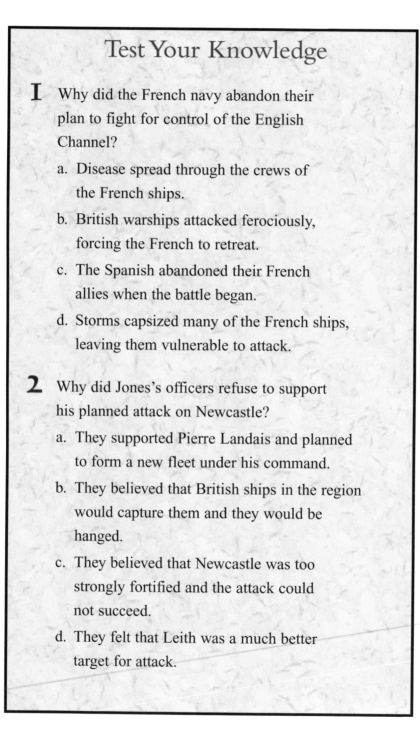

Test Your Knowledge

1 Why did the French navy abandon their plan to fight for control of the English Channel?

   a. Disease spread through the crews of the French ships.

   b. British warships attacked ferociously, forcing the French to retreat.

   c. The Spanish abandoned their French allies when the battle began.

   d. Storms capsized many of the French ships, leaving them vulnerable to attack.

2 Why did Jones's officers refuse to support his planned attack on Newcastle?

   a. They supported Pierre Landais and planned to form a new fleet under his command.

   b. They believed that British ships in the region would capture them and they would be hanged.

   c. They believed that Newcastle was too strongly fortified and the attack could not succeed.

   d. They felt that Leith was a much better target for attack.

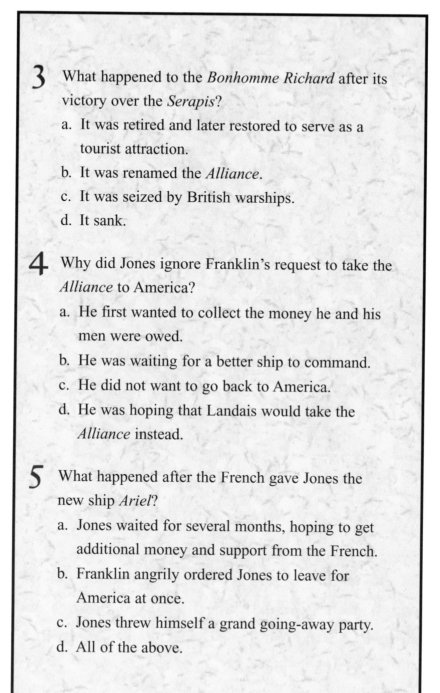

3 What happened to the *Bonhomme Richard* after its victory over the *Serapis*?

a. It was retired and later restored to serve as a tourist attraction.

b. It was renamed the *Alliance*.

c. It was seized by British warships.

d. It sank.

4 Why did Jones ignore Franklin's request to take the *Alliance* to America?

a. He first wanted to collect the money he and his men were owed.

b. He was waiting for a better ship to command.

c. He did not want to go back to America.

d. He was hoping that Landais would take the *Alliance* instead.

5 What happened after the French gave Jones the new ship *Ariel*?

a. Jones waited for several months, hoping to get additional money and support from the French.

b. Franklin angrily ordered Jones to leave for America at once.

c. Jones threw himself a grand going-away party.

d. All of the above.

ANSWERS: 1. a; 2. b; 3. d; 4. a; 5. d

War's End

After almost three years' absence, John Paul Jones finally set off for America on the *Ariel* on October 7, 1780. His men had loaded his ship full of gunpowder and weapons. At last, the American army would soon receive the supplies from Europe it desperately needed.

But the *Ariel* ran into trouble just days after leaving the French port of L'Orient. A great storm blew up, making the ship rattle and rock furiously from side to side. Jones was used to storms at sea, but he had never seen anything like this. He had no choice but to turn back toward France. As the winds grew stronger, Jones feared that the ship would capsize. He and his terrified crew doubted that they would live to see land again.

Jones remained calm, as he so often did in a crisis. Fighting the heavy rains and winds, he carefully navigated the *Ariel* back to L'Orient. By the time the ship reached port, it was badly damaged and many of the provisions it carried were destroyed. However, everyone aboard had survived, and they knew that they owed their lives to Jones.

Jones hoped that he would be rewarded with a better ship. Instead, the French authorities left him in command of the *Ariel.* Aboard the patched-up ship, Jones once again sailed off for America on December 18. This time, the trip was uneventful until he reached the West Indies, where he encountered the *Triumph,* a ship crewed by Americans loyal to the British. Jones

Jones consistently displayed nerves of steel in battle, whether engaging in hand-to-hand combat on board ship or masquerading as a British captain to fool an opponent.

sized up the enemy ship, which he determined was faster and better armed than the *Ariel.*

Jones's first choice was to flee, but he suspected the slower *Ariel* would be quickly overtaken. Instead, he decided to trick the *Triumph.* He had a British flag hoisted above the *Ariel* and appeared on the deck in a British captain's uniform. Moving the *Ariel* within about 30 feet of the enemy ship, he called out to its captain, John Pindar, asking for news of the war. The two captains chatted for a while, until Pindar grew suspicious of Jones's behavior. Jones then shouted to his men to open fire. They hammered the *Triumph* for about ten minutes before Pindar surrendered. However, Pindar managed to sail the *Triumph* away, and the *Ariel* was too slow to stop her. Jones was furious that he had won the battle but still lost his prize.

For the rest of the voyage, Jones avoided any more encounters with British ships. On February 18, 1781, the *Ariel* safely arrived in Philadelphia. There, hundreds of barrels of precious gunpowder were unloaded and readied for transport to General George Washington's troops.

At first, Jones received a hero's welcome. He was particularly gratified by a grand reception during which he was greeted by members of Congress and many other leading citizens in the city. However, his moment of glory quickly soured. People began asking why it had taken so long for Jones to return to America with his precious cargo. Many called for Congress to launch an investigation into the matter.

With his dallying in Paris, Jones was, of course, at least partly responsible for the delay. During the investigation, however, he was able to deflect all blame onto a convenient scapegoat—his longtime enemy Pierre Landais. After Landais defied Jones's authority and set sail on the *Alliance* to America, he had a mental breakdown. By the time he reached Philadelphia, he had to be carried off his ship, kicking and screaming. Conveniently for Jones, Landais's behavior made it easy for Congress to believe that he was solely at fault.

WAITING FOR A SHIP

Jones had more difficulty persuading Congress to give him what he truly wanted—the rank of admiral. Other captains, perhaps jealous of his battle exploits, spread enough rumors about Jones to foil his promotion. The navy offered him the next best thing: command of the *America,* which was to be the grandest ship in the

American navy. Jones rushed to Portsmouth, where the *America* was being built.

To his disappointment, Jones found construction on the *America* was moving slowly. Even worse, the shipbuilders did not seem to have enough iron, wood, or even workers to complete it. Strapped for money, Congress was not providing the funds needed to finish the project. Anxious for his ship, Jones paid some carpenters out of his own pocket, but this did little to speed the construction.

News of the war's progress only added to his desperation. In October 1781, the British general Charles Cornwallis had surrendered his army to Washington in Yorkville, Virginia. While Jones was happy to hear of the American victory, it suggested that the war, and Jones's chance to further distinguish himself in battle, was coming to an end.

Increasing his frustration, Jones learned that Congress had decided to give the half-finished *America* to the French. Once again, Jones had no ship. With little hope for another command soon, Jones took a drastic step. With the permission of Congress, he decided to volunteer for the French navy. The French had a fleet of 70 ships that was leaving Boston for

British-held Jamaica. Jones offered his services as a pilot, since he knew the waters off Jamaica well from his days of working on slave ships. The French welcomed him aboard *Le Triumphant,* the greatest ship in the fleet. But before the ship could reach Jamaica, news came that the war was over. The American rebels had finally defeated the British.

A NEW DIRECTION

Jones celebrated the revolution's success as a great moment for the American people and was gratified by his part in making it happen. But the end of the war was difficult for Jones. He was unsure what to do next. As Jones often did in times of uncertainty, he considered giving up the sea and settling down. In a letter to a friend, Jones wrote, "I wish to establish myself on a place of my own and to offer my hand to some fair daughter of Liberty."[13]

At the same time, Jones's ambition pulled him in another direction. He saw that the new United States of America needed a powerful navy. In his opinion, he was the best man to build and manage it. Jones had a vision of the United States as a great naval power. To make that happen, he proposed establishing a naval academy, creating a corps of talented officers, and building a fleet of ships that could rival Britain's. However, Congress lacked sufficient funds and interest in Jones's grand scheme. Instead of building up the American navy, it was busy selling the few ships it had to raise some quick cash.

Reluctantly, Jones had to settle for a much less interesting mission. He received Congress's approval to return to Paris to pressure the French government into paying the prize money still owed to the crews of the *Ranger* and *Bonhomme Richard.* In return for his work as a prize agent, Congress agreed to pay Jones's expenses and his captain's salary.

As in the past, living in Paris gave Jones the opportunity to socialize with the French elite. Over the next three years there, he again met with King Louis XVI and had a romance with an English widow. But his work in Paris proved tedious. He described getting the prize money as a "difficult and disagreeable task."[14] Jones was no doubt also disappointed that the king did not give him a high post in the French navy.

Feeling that there was nothing left for him in France, Jones returned to America in the summer of 1787. On this visit, Congress awarded him a gold medal, which he treasured. But the honor did little to resolve his biggest problem—what to do with the rest of his life.

Qualifications of a Naval Officer

For more than one hundred years, midshipmen at the U.S. Naval Academy have memorized "Qualifications of a Naval Officer"—a three-paragraph summary of the personal characteristics required of an officer of the U.S. Navy. According to the statement, "It is by no means enough that an officer of the Navy should be a capable mariner. He must be that, of course, but also a great deal more. He should be as well a gentleman of liberal education, refined manners, punctilious courtesy, and the nicest sense of personal honor." Perhaps most important to students was the "Qualifications" conclusion: "In one word, every commander should keep constantly before him the great truth, that to be well obeyed, he must be perfectly esteemed."[*]

Each class of midshipmen was taught that these were the words of John Paul Jones, who by that time was regarded as the father of the American navy. In 1986, however, naval historian James C. Bradford made a conclusive case that Jones was not their actual author. "Qualifications" was, in fact, written in 1900, more than

In November, on the streets of New York, Jones encountered a part of his past he would have been happy to have been rid of forever. While talking to

one hundred years after Jones's death, by journalist Augustus C. Buell. He was author of the two-volume biography *Paul Jones: Founder of the American Navy.* Drawing from snippets of Jones's letters, as well as other sources, Buell came up with "Qualifications" and passed it off as Jones's own work.

Not everyone in the navy was happy about Bradford's revelation. Naval officers had long embraced the "Qualifications." Wanting to see themselves not just as officers, but also as gentlemen, they found its words so inspiring that they were hesitant to admit that their authorship was part of a journalist's hoax. It was not until 2003 that the navy officially addressed the controversy. The text, as printed in the student handbook *Reef Points,* is now attributed to "Augustus C. Buell in 1900 to reflect his views of John Paul Jones."**

* *Proceedings of the United States Naval Institute* 129, Issue 10 (October 2003), 98.

** Lori Lyn Bogle and Ensign Joel I. Holwitt, "The Best Quote Jones Never Wrote," *Naval History* 18, Issue 2 (April 2004), 12.

a friend, Jones was accosted by Pierre Landais. According to Landais's account, he spit in Jones's face and challenged him to a duel. Jones wanted to avoid the fight. As rumors spread about the incident, he said to the press that Landais had never really spit at him, since the spitting would have constituted a challenge only a coward would ignore. Landais, though, would not let the matter go. In a letter to a New York newspaper, Landais wrote, "I do hereby certify, to the public, that I really, and in fact, spit all the spittle I could spare out of my mouth then, out of contempt, in the face of John Paul, or Paul Jones."[15]

Perhaps Jones could not deal with another run-in with the unbalanced Landais. Perhaps he came to suspect that, however celebrated he was, there was no place for him in the United States. Perhaps he thought that, despite his many disappointments there, Europe still promised his best chance at a glorious future. Whatever his reasoning, two days after the Landais affair, John Paul Jones boarded a ship bound for France.

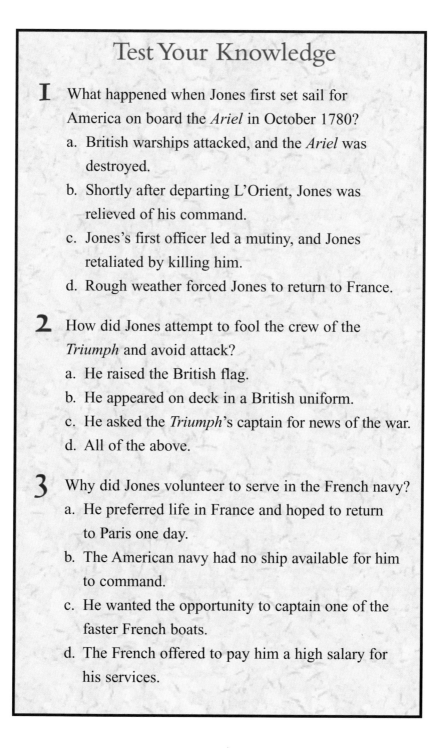

Test Your Knowledge

I What happened when Jones first set sail for America on board the *Ariel* in October 1780?

   a. British warships attacked, and the *Ariel* was destroyed.

   b. Shortly after departing L'Orient, Jones was relieved of his command.

   c. Jones's first officer led a mutiny, and Jones retaliated by killing him.

   d. Rough weather forced Jones to return to France.

2 How did Jones attempt to fool the crew of the *Triumph* and avoid attack?

   a. He raised the British flag.

   b. He appeared on deck in a British uniform.

   c. He asked the *Triumph*'s captain for news of the war.

   d. All of the above.

3 Why did Jones volunteer to serve in the French navy?

   a. He preferred life in France and hoped to return to Paris one day.

   b. The American navy had no ship available for him to command.

   c. He wanted the opportunity to captain one of the faster French boats.

   d. The French offered to pay him a high salary for his services.

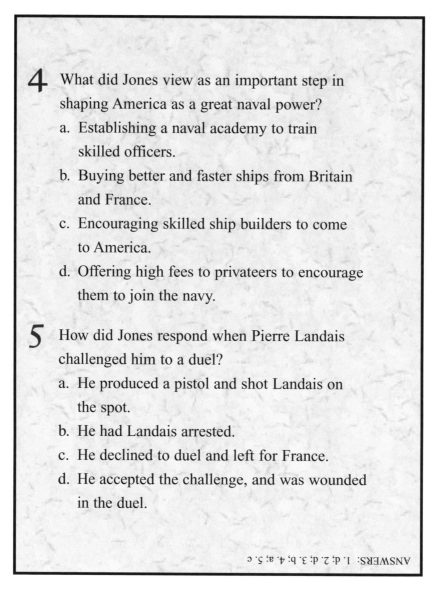

4 What did Jones view as an important step in shaping America as a great naval power?

   a. Establishing a naval academy to train skilled officers.

   b. Buying better and faster ships from Britain and France.

   c. Encouraging skilled ship builders to come to America.

   d. Offering high fees to privateers to encourage them to join the navy.

5 How did Jones respond when Pierre Landais challenged him to a duel?

   a. He produced a pistol and shot Landais on the spot.

   b. He had Landais arrested.

   c. He declined to duel and left for France.

   d. He accepted the challenge, and was wounded in the duel.

ANSWERS: 1. d; 2. d; 3. b; 4. a; 5. c

Final Days

S oon after John Paul Jones arrived in Paris, he received an
  intriguing proposal. Thomas Jefferson, the American
ambassador in France, told Jones that Catherine, Tsarina of
Russia, was interested in hiring him. The Russian navy was
in disrepair. She needed a commander to bring it into shape
and thought Jones was the man for the job.

After his service to the American navy had ended, Jones was hired
by the Russian navy to aid in their campaign against the Turks.

At first, Jones did not take the offer seriously. He still hoped that the new United States would commit itself to building a navy and place him in charge of it. But a meeting with a Russian ambassador helped change Jones's mind. Always susceptible to flattery, Jones delighted in the ambassador's effusive praise of his talents. It was enough to convince Jones that in Russia he might find the recognition he craved.

In early 1788, Jones set off for St. Petersburg, the Russian capital. The trip was very difficult. After weeks of traveling through ice and snow, Jones arrived in the city feeling exhausted and sick. Instead of taking time to recover, he plunged into the luxurious world of the Russian court. Catherine invited Jones to her palace and seemed impressed with him. She wrote to her military adviser, Grigori Potemkin, that "this man is extremely capable of multiplying fear and trembling in his foe."[16]

The foes Catherine had in mind were the Turks. For 300 years, the Turks had controlled the city of Constantinople. Catherine hoped to seize the city for Russia. Her first step toward that end was to gain control of the Black Sea. To do so, Catherine needed the Russian navy to destroy a Turkish fleet stationed there.

Jones was given command of 12 armed ships to fight the Turks. The most impressive was the *Vladimir.* Backing up these ships was a flotilla, or small fleet, of about 25 small vessels. Most were galleys, which were propelled through the water using oars.

Jones knew that the mission would not be easy. The Turks not only had more and better ships. Their fleet also had a great commander, Ghazi Hassan-Pasha, with a well-earned reputation for ruthlessness. Jones developed a careful strategy to take on the superior fleet. He planned to situate his ships in the Liman, an arm of the Black Sea at the mouth of the Dniper River. Jones hoped to lure the slow-moving Turkish fleet into the Liman, where both his warships and the galleys would pound it with gunfire.

Executing the plan would be tricky. One problem was that the waters of the Liman were not very deep. Jones and his captains would have to be careful not to let their ships get stuck in banks of mud and sand. But Jones faced an even greater obstacle. The flotilla of small ships was not under his direct command. Instead, it was led by Charles, Prince of Nassau-Siegen. From the moment they met, Jones saw that working with this German prince would be nearly impossible. Nassau-Siegen was inept, dishonest, and interested only in his personal gain.

A BATTLE IN THE LIMAN

Jones's fleet had its first encounter with the enemy on June 5, 1788, when a few Turkish ships entered the Liman. That night, Nassau-Siegen was charged with sneaking a few small ships behind the Turkish vessels to cut off their escape route once the battle started. But the Turks saw them coming and began to fire. Nassau-Siegen made a hasty retreat.

The real battle came two days later, when dozens of Turkish ships descended on Jones's fleet. He ordered his ships to form a v-shape, so that as they sailed forward they could fire on the Turks from two sides. Almost immediately, the men on many of the small Russian ships panicked and fled. Among them was Nassau-Siegen. Even without these ships, the Russians led by Jones managed to set two Turkish vessels on fire. Sensing that they were losing the battle, the Turkish fleet withdrew.

The fight was a small victory for Jones. But Nassau-Siegen immediately sent letters to Potemkin, claiming that he was the real hero. In his version of the battle,

Jones had hung back, too afraid to take on the mighty Turks. Jones learned of Nassau-Siegen's false claims, but he was hesitant to accuse Nassau-Siegen of lying. Knowing that Pasha's fleet would soon return, ready for another fight, Jones decided that the best way to challenge Nassau-Siegen's lies was to again prove his own worth in battle.

As Jones had predicted, the Turkish fleet came back to the Liman on June 16. The Turks beat drums and shouted threats, hoping that the sight of their powerful fleet would frighten the Russians into a retreat. Pasha steered his ship toward the *Vladimir,* eager to do battle with Jones himself. But it ran into a sandbank and became stuck. With Pasha's ship out of commission, the other Turkish captains, unsure of what to do, stopped their approach.

Jones saw a chance to go on the offensive. The next morning, he initiated a full-scale attack. As the Russian ships plowed toward them, the Turks made a frenzied retreat. With victory assured, Jones ordered the *Vladimir* to head toward Pasha's grounded ship, which he wanted to seize as a prize. But before the *Vladimir* reached its prey, the ship's captain, Panaiotti Alexiano, had its men drop the *Vladimir*'s anchor, leaving Jones's ship unable to move forward. At the same time, Nassau-Siegen appeared in his yacht to claim Pasha's ship. Jones lost his prize but he won the battle, forcing the Turks once again to withdraw.

Having escaped from his grounded ship, Pasha was still determined to defeat the Russian force. He instructed his largest ships to slip into the Liman. Nine of them quickly ran aground, spelling disaster for the Turks. Nassau-Siegen wanted to take out his flotilla and burn the grounded ships, but Jones argued against the action. The Turks still had smaller ships that might overtake Jones's fleet if Nassau-Siegen's flotilla was away. The discussion turned into a heated argument. The next morning, completely ignoring Jones's concerns, Nassau-Siegen led his entire small fleet to the grounded ships. He set them ablaze, burning to death nearly 2,000 Turkish sailors and slaves in the process.

Jones had one final encounter with the Turkish fleet. On July 1, Pasha's remaining ships arrived in the Liman. This time, Jones took a small boat, sailed ahead of the rest of the Russian ships, and rammed it straight into the first Turkish galley he reached. The Turks were overwhelmed and surrendered. Jones wanted to take Pasha's galley as a prize, but Alexiano set it on fire before he could.

A SCANDAL IN ST. PETERSBURG

The naval campaign against the Turks was over, and the Russians had triumphed. But Jones received no credit for the victory. Nassau-Siegen managed to convince the Russian leaders that he alone was responsible for the successful campaign. For his part in the mission, the prince was rewarded with a huge estate and a gold sword covered with diamonds. Jones received only a small medal.

In November, Jones returned to St. Petersburg. Although in bad health, he filled his days devising new campaigns for the Russian navy. Tsarina Catherine showed no interest in his plans. Jones was ignored by Russian society until the following April, when he was accused of assaulting a ten-year-old girl. The charges were eventually dropped, but Jones's reputation was damaged. Catherine placed him on leave from the Russian navy.

Jones left Russia in the summer of 1789, with no particular destination in mind. He spent a year wandering through Europe before settling in Paris in May 1790. By that time, France was engulfed in its own revolution, and most of his old friends among the nobility had fled the country. Lonely and bored, Jones repeatedly wrote letters to Catherine in Russia, hoping somehow to return to her good graces. However, his health was poor, and he was no longer physically able to serve in any navy. Coming upon Jones in Paris, the English writer Thomas Carlyle reported, "In faded naval uniform, Paul Jones lingers visible here; like a wine skin from which the wine is drawn. Like the ghost of himself!" [17]

DEATH OF A HERO

On July 18, 1792, Jones sent an urgent note to Gouverneur Morris, the American ambassador in Paris. Jones told him that he was dying and needed Morris's help in writing his will. Morris visited the ailing Jones that day, then went to check on him late that night, only to find that Jones had died.

A few days later, a letter arrived at Jones's house. It contained a proposal from Thomas Jefferson. Congress was putting together a delegation to negotiate the release of American sailors taken prisoner off the

Burying John Paul Jones

Soon after John Paul Jones's death, the French government, at its own expense, took over his funeral arrangements. Believing that the United States might want his body returned to America for burial, French representatives preserved his body in alcohol and laid his remains in a lead coffin. But the United States seemed uninterested in Jones's remains, so the French eventually buried him in a small cemetery in Paris.

In the century after his death, Jones was largely forgotten by history. He was regarded as little more than a footnote in the story of the American Revolution. But in the early twentieth century, there was a sudden revival of interest in Jones. President Theodore Roosevelt was particularly fascinated by the American Revolution's greatest naval hero. He was trying to build a great fleet of warships that would be commanded by an elite, professional corps of naval officers. Roosevelt thought that by promoting John Paul Jones as a great American hero, he could gain support for his plans.

Roosevelt's efforts were aided by Charles D. Sigbec, a former general who became the American ambassador to France in 1899. Sigbec was obsessed with finding the grave of John Paul Jones. He wanted to bring the bones of the legendary commander back to the United States. After six years, he succeeded in locating Jones's remains. Roosevelt sent a squadron of American ships to Paris to retrieve them in 1905. The president planned a grand ceremony for the next year on April 24, the anniversary of Jones's capture of the British warship the *Drake*. Finally, Jones's corpse was laid to rest at the U.S. Naval Academy in Annapolis, Maryland.

Still, the navy was not satisfied with the wooden vault that held his coffin. Congress eventually approved more than $100,000 for a huge marble crypt. Its design was inspired by the tomb of the great French general and emperor Napoleon Bonaparte. Since that time, thousands of visitors have viewed Jones's tomb every year. Recently, the centennial anniversary of his reburial was celebrated in Annapolis.

After the Revolutionary War, Jones proposed establishing an American naval academy to train a corps of talented officers. It would be many years before Jones's vision of the United States Naval Academy became reality; today its graduates help fulfill his dream of making America a great naval power.

Barbary Coast of Africa. As Secretary of State, Jefferson wanted Jones to head the group. With his death, Jones lost this final opportunity to restore his reputation and once again serve the American government.

Two years later, Congress finally realized the need for a military presence at sea. It commissioned the construction of six warships. Three of these—the *United*

States, the *Constitution,* and the *Constellation*—were eventually built. Their construction marks the beginning of the modern American navy.

Ironically, the decision came too late for John Paul Jones, who would have loved nothing more than to command this new fleet and oversee the navy's growth. Even without his active leadership, the American navy flourished over time. True to Jones's impassioned prediction, the U.S. Navy truly has become "the wonder and envy of the world."[18]

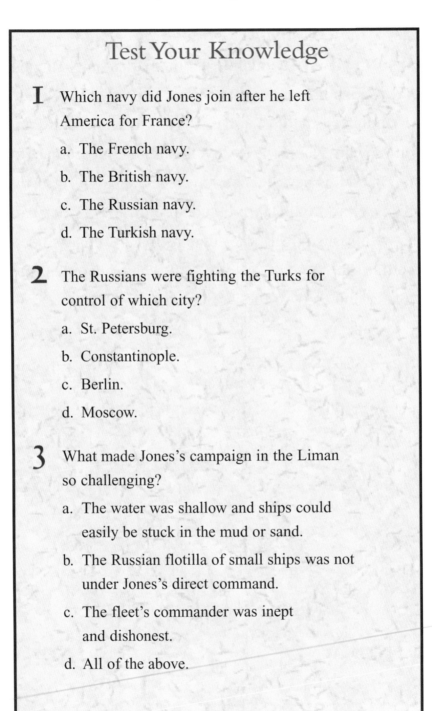

Test Your Knowledge

1 Which navy did Jones join after he left America for France?

    a. The French navy.

    b. The British navy.

    c. The Russian navy.

    d. The Turkish navy.

2 The Russians were fighting the Turks for control of which city?

    a. St. Petersburg.

    b. Constantinople.

    c. Berlin.

    d. Moscow.

3 What made Jones's campaign in the Liman so challenging?

    a. The water was shallow and ships could easily be stuck in the mud or sand.

    b. The Russian flotilla of small ships was not under Jones's direct command.

    c. The fleet's commander was inept and dishonest.

    d. All of the above.

4 Why did Jones not receive credit for the Russian naval victory in the Liman?

  a. He had lost favor with the Tsarina and she dismissed him.

  b. A German prince claimed responsibility for the victory.

  c. A Russian commander claimed credit for the naval successes.

  d. The Turks never surrendered and the campaign was ultimately a failure.

5 Jones died before he could learn of a proposal from Thomas Jefferson for a new opportunity to serve the American government. What was it?

  a. Jones was asked to head a delegation negotiating the release of American sailors taken prisoner near the African coast.

  b. Jones was asked to chair a commission studying the plans for an American naval academy.

  c. Jones was asked to review plans for a new fleet of battleships.

  d. Jones was asked to serve as the American ambassador to France.

ANSWERS: 1. c; 2. b; 3. d; 4. b; 5. a

1747   John Paul is born at Arbigland in Scotland on July 6.

1760   Paul goes to sea as an apprentice aboard the *Friendship*.

1764   Paul is hired as the third mate on the slave ship
        King George.

1770   Paul becomes a freemason at Bernard's Lodge in
        Kirkcudbright, Scotland.

1772   In June Paul is cleared of charges in Tobago relating
        to the death of Mungo Maxwell.

1773   Paul flees the West Indies after being accused of murder.

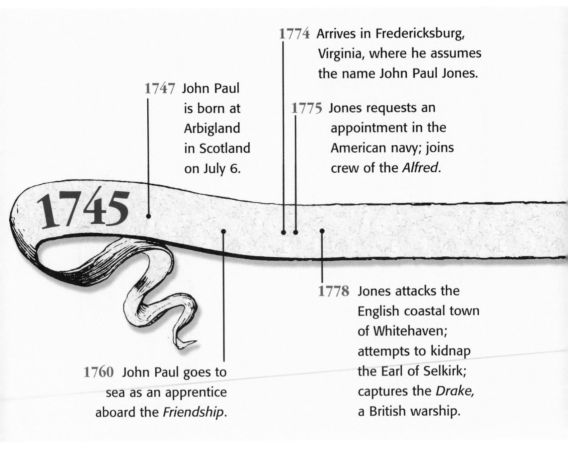

1747 John Paul
     is born at
     Arbigland
     in Scotland
     on July 6.

1774 Arrives in Fredericksburg,
     Virginia, where he assumes
     the name John Paul Jones.

1775 Jones requests an
     appointment in the
     American navy; joins
     crew of the *Alfred*.

1745

1760 John Paul goes to
     sea as an apprentice
     aboard the *Friendship*.

1778 Jones attacks the
     English coastal town
     of Whitehaven;
     attempts to kidnap
     the Earl of Selkirk;
     captures the *Drake*,
     a British warship.

1774 Paul arrives in Fredericksburg, Virginia, where he assumes the name John Paul Jones.

1775 Jones requests an appointment in the American navy; joins crew of the *Alfred*.

1776 Jones battles the *Glasgow*; is given command of the *Providence*; takes 16 prizes during a seven-week mission.

1777 Jones arrives in Portsmouth, New Hampshire, to take command of the French ship *Amphitrite*, but instead is assigned to the *Ranger*; sails the *Ranger* to France.

1779 *Bonhomme Richard* defeats the British warship the *Serapis* in battle; Jones sails the *Serapis* to Holland.

1792 Jones dies in France at the age of 45 on July 18.

1783 The American Revolution formally ends in September with the signing of the Treaty of Paris.

1795

1780 Jones arrives in France, where he is celebrated as a war hero.

1788 Jones joins the Russian navy; defeats Turkish fleet in the Battles of the Liman.

1778 Jones attacks the English coastal town of Whitehaven; attempts to kidnap the Earl of Selkirk; captures the *Drake,* a British warship.

1779 Jones takes command of the *Bonhomme Richard* in February; the *Bonhomme Richard* defeats the British warship the *Serapis* in battle; Jones sails the *Serapis* to Holland.

1780 Jones arrives in France in February, where he is celebrated as a war hero; in December Jones sails for America aboard the *Ariel.*

1781 Jones travels to Portsmouth to take command of the *America,* which is instead given to the French navy.

1782 Jones joins the French navy as a pilot.

1783 Jones sails to France in November, charged by Congress with collecting prize money for his crews.

1788 Jones arrives in St. Petersburg to join the Russian navy; defeats Turkish fleet in the Battles of the Liman.

1790 Jones returns to Paris; rejects a military commission from George Washington due to illness.

1792 Jones dies in France at the age of 45 on July 18.

1905 Jones's body is interred at the U.S. Naval Academy in Annapolis, Maryland.

2005 The U.S. Naval Academy celebrates the centennial of the transfer of Jones's remains to the United States.

Notes

CHAPTER 1
A Duel at Sea

1. Evan Thomas, *John Paul Jones: Sailor, Hero, Father of the American Navy* (New York: Simon and Schuster, 2003), 180.

2. Ibid., 186.

3. Ibid., 192.

CHAPTER 2
A Sailor's Life

4. Samuel Eliot Morison, *John Paul Jones: A Sailor's Biography* (Boston: Little, Brown and Company, 1959), 7.

5. Thomas, *John Paul Jones,* 26.

6. Ibid., 16.

CHAPTER 3
Joining the Revolution

7. Morison, *John Paul Jones*, 62.

8. Thomas, *John Paul Jones,* 77.

CHAPTER 4
On the *Ranger*

9. Morison, *John Paul Jones,* 109.

CHAPTER 5
Itching for a Fight

10. Thomas, *John Paul Jones*, 135.

11. Ibid., 156.

CHAPTER 6
A Naval Hero

12. Ibid., 203.

CHAPTER 7
War's End

13. Ibid., 257.

14. Ibid., 262.

15. Ibid., 265.

CHAPTER 8
Final Days

16. Thomas, *John Paul Jones,* 274.

17. Ibid., 302.

18. Ibid., 156.

Bogle, Lori Lyn, and Ensign Joel I. Holwitt. "The Best Quote Jones Never Wrote." *Naval History* Volume 18, Issue 2 (April 2004).

Fowler, William M., Jr. *Rebels Under Sail: The American Navy During the Revolution.* New York: Charles Scribner's Sons, 1976.

Hallas, James Harry. "The Search for John Paul Jones." *American History* Volume 32, Issue 3 (July/August 1997).

Morison, Samuel Eliot. *John Paul Jones: A Sailor's Biography.* Boston: Little, Brown, 1959.

Proceedings of the United States Naval Institute Volume 129, Issue 10 (October 2003).

Thomas, Evan. *John Paul Jones: Sailor, Hero, Father of the American Navy.* New York: Simon and Schuster, 2003.

Biesty, Stephen, and Richard Platt. *Man-of-War.* New York: Dorling Kindersley, 1993.

Haugen, Brenda, and Andrew Santella. *John Paul Jones: Father of the American Navy.* Minneapolis, Minn.: Compass Point Books, 2005.

Murray, Aaron R., ed. *American Revolution Battles and Leaders.* New York: DK Publishing, 2004.

Simmons, Clara Ann. *John Paul Jones: America's Sailor.* Annapolis, Md.: Naval Institute Press, 1997.

———. *The Story of the U.S. Naval Academy.* Annapolis, Md.: Naval Institute Press, 1995.

Smolinski, Diane. *Naval Warfare of the Revolutionary War.* Chicago: Heinemann Library, 2002.

WEBSITES

John Paul Jones Cottage Museum
www.jpj.demon.co.uk

Naval Historical Center
www.history.navy.mil

Naval War College Museum
www.nwc.navy.mil/museum

United States Naval Academy Museum
www.nadn.navy.mil/Museum

USS John Paul Jones Association
www.ussjohnpauljones.org

Index

LIZ SONNEBORN is a writer living in Brooklyn, New York. A graduate of Swarthmore College, she has written more than 50 books for children and adults, including *The American West*, *A to Z of American Women in the Performing Arts*, and *The New York Public Library's Amazing Native American History*, winner of a 2000 Parent's Choice Award.